D0564843

The Teacher's
Guide to
Winning
Grants

DATE DUE

DISCARD

DEMCO, INC. 38-2931

The Teacher's Guide to Winning Grants

David G. Bauer

Jossey-Bass Publishers • San Francisco

This edition copyright © 1999 by Jossey-Bass Inc., Publishers, 350 Sansome Street, San Francisco, California 94104. Previous version copyright © 1994 by Scholastic Inc.

All rights reserved. No part of this publication may be reproduced, stored in a retrieval system, or transmitted, in any form or by any means, electronic, mechanical, photocopying, recording, or otherwise, without the prior written permission of Jossey-Bass Inc., Publishers. Jossey-Bass books and products are available through most bookstores. To contact Jossey-Bass directly, call (888) 378-2537, fax to (800) 605-2665, or visit our website at www.josseybass.com.

Substantial discounts on bulk quantities of Jossey-Bass books are available to corporations, professional associations, and other organizations. For details and discount information, contact the special sales department at Jossey-Bass.

Interior design by Bruce Lundquist.

Manufactured in the United States of America.

Library of Congress Cataloging-in-Publication Data

Bauer, David G.
    The teacher's guide to winning grants / David G. Bauer.—1st ed.
        p.   cm.
    Rev. ed. of: Grantseeking primer for classroom leaders. c1994.
    Includes bibliographical references.
    ISBN 0-7879-4493-9
    1. Educational fund raising—United States—Handbooks, manuals, etc.
2. Teaching—United States—Finance—Handbooks, manuals, etc.   3. Education—
Research grants—United States—Handbooks, manuals, etc.   4. Proposal writing
in education—United States—Handbooks, manuals, etc.   5. Proposal writing for
grants—United States—Handbooks, manuals, etc.   I. Bauer, David G.   Grantseeking primer for classroom leaders.   II. Title.
LC243.A1B37   1999   98-44021
379.1'3 — dc21

FIRST EDITION
PB Printing   10 9 8 7 6 5 4 3 2 1

Contents

Exhibits, Figures, and Tables

Introduction

SUCCESSFUL GRANTSEEKING is one of the foremost vehicles for developing, enhancing, and delivering your classroom's educational programs. Seeking grant funds for elementary and middle school education is in itself a positive process because the need flows from a desire to implement a proposed project, change or develop a program, procure equipment, or, in some cases, evaluate or perform research that will benefit education. However, seeking grants solely for the sake of bringing money into a school can result in confusion and rapid, erratic changes in your educational focus. Money, be it grant funds or any other, does not ensure that education will be advanced. Increased funding for education does not guarantee improved educational experiences or learning outcomes. Educators, administrators, and taxpayers are aware that increasing school budgets and raising taxes to support education do not necessarily mean that educational programs will be improved, that parents and the community will become involved, or that children will learn. But if an educator is willing to make the effort to work with a community advisory committee to develop a grant proposal, participants are more likely to use the resources resulting from their hard work to effect change and improve the educational atmosphere. Use the grantseeking techniques presented in this primer and you will increase your grant's success and enhance your educational programs. You will also be rewarded with the following:

- Solutions to your school's problems
- An increase in school and community involvement
- More successful ways to use volunteers
- An increase in the number of parents and children involved in the development and use of educational resources

Many grantseekers get started improperly. They focus on technology needs, equipment, and software. Although grantors may allow and even encourage the incorporation of technology into grant proposals, they view it as a means to an end. They want to take credit for increased learning, not items purchased from a school's technology equipment list. Remember, improved learning and student achievement are the genesis for grantseeking, and these changes cost money to implement and to support.

Most people in my age group (forty-five to fifty-five) who have been involved in education for twenty years or more are skeptical of individuals, groups, or programs that espouse educational change that is unaccompanied by an increase in funds to support new and improved programs. We have witnessed many innovations that demonstrated positive educational outcomes. But because the funds subsidized only a model project, not the program's operation or replication, the program never materialized. Money and resources alone do not ensure a great educational program, but they are the basis for sustained change and improvement once a program is proven worthwhile. Parents and school administrators must realize that grant monies increase the rate of educational improvement. Carrying on valid educational improvements and making them available to more students should be the work of taxes and levies, not increased grantseeking. Your school district must realize that some of the programs started with grant monies will require other forms of support once the grant is completed and the methodology proven worthwhile.

It is important to note the difference here between grantseeking and fund-raising. Grantseeking is one way of raising funds. A proposal for a grant is an outline of an agreement to address a particular situation by means of prescribed steps. Fund-raising uses a variety of techniques to encourage donors to give money to an organization and a cause. Money gained from fund-raising can be used for the general support of a school's mission. Almost anything that enhances education can be supported by monies raised in a general fund-raising appeal. However, grantseeking is based on prescribed activities that are supposed to bring about results in a specific area of education. For example, educators are forced to seek grant funds for materials and equipment that are impossible to obtain through budgets or other general fund-development sources (parent-teacher groups and so on). Grantseeking provides an answer to the problem of resource development in our nation's elementary and middle schools, but it is difficult if not inappropriate to use grants for the continuation of programs.

By reading this primer, you will learn how and when to employ the grants mechanism to get funds to help you reach your classroom's educational goals and objectives, acquire materials and equipment, and move your school in the direction you want.

It is best when your educational system, whether it consists of one site or an entire district, is willing to support your grants effort. But your school district must realize that some of the programs started with grant monies will require other forms of support once the grant is completed and the methodology proven worthwhile.

Too many school systems encourage classroom leaders to invest their out-of-school and spare time to pursue grants and then get cold feet when they are asked for matching funds and in-kind contributions or are shown a formula to increase the school's commitment to the project over a given period of time. Even when the proposal seems simple and the benefits obvious—such as getting a grant for five new classroom computers—issues such as who pays for the software, maintenance, and storage need to be addressed before the proposal is submitted and the hardware arrives. The adage "you don't get something for nothing" rings true in the educational grants arena. Gifts and grants have many hidden costs that need to be addressed in advance of proposal submission.

This primer describes grantseeking techniques that will increase your chances for success and provides you with a time-efficient proposal development system. As a former K–12 educator and administrator, I know firsthand the pressures and demands on the educator's time. Therefore, I also know that before you invest your valuable time in a grantseeking venture, you must know what works.

The key to implementing my systematic approach to grantseeking is understanding that the process parallels the development of superior educational achievement and is based on the school community's involvement. From developing fundable ideas to incorporating an information system that ascertains who can help us get our foot in the door with a funding source, the system works because of the commitment and involvement of volunteers—be they parents, friends of education, graduates, or even students themselves.

This book provides you, the classroom leader, with a time-efficient method that helps you mobilize your resources to organize your proposal ideas, write a cogent and effective proposal, obtain grant funds, and experience the fun and excitement of implementing your proposal.

The formula for grants success is shown in the figure on the next page. Grantseeking provides the catalyst in this equation. Change occurs at an increased rate.

Remember that grant money is neither the end nor the beginning of a quest. It is the catalyst in a formula. Set up properly, a grants system leads

---

FORMULA FOR SUCCESSFUL GRANTSEEKING

Needs	+	Solutions	+	Commitment	=	Educational Advancement
of your students, classroom, community, and society		ideas and strategies to adapt change, strengthen the education system		the extra effort of you, your colleagues, and parents	∞*	new strategies, equipment, and materials to meet the challenges of education

*Grantseeking provides the catalyst in this equation. Change occurs at an increased rate.

---

to positive outcomes even without that catalyst. When an idea-generating and problem-solving system is developed with positive outcomes as the desired result, the classroom, school, and community will move in that positive direction. However, progress will be slow if the catalyst—money—is not there. In contrast, school communities that continually focus on what is wrong (that is, on what they don't have) stagnate, or even deteriorate, and find it difficult to generate excitement about their projects.

Some educators believe that money alone is the answer and that an increase in resources will solve education's problems. However, having more catalyst than necessary does not increase the speed or strength of the reaction or produce the desired results. The proper equation needs balance—balance that can occur only when the correct amount of each component is used.

You, the classroom leader, control the chemistry and must keep the balance of the equation in mind. A grants system can depend too much on the supervisor or administration. Quality ideas and educational solutions spring from an environment that questions what works, why it works, and how to make it work better. It takes parents, teachers, school staff, and a supportive administration to make a grants effort succeed, but the classroom leader is the basic element.

Novice grantseekers mistakenly assume that the school should provide someone to write their ideas into a proposal. That seldom works. You probably do not need or want anyone else to write your proposal, but you may need internal support services. Contact your district office and supervisor to determine what assistance the district can provide and to ensure that you follow all district procedures and rules.

Jossey-Bass and Bauer Associates have produced a guide for grants success for principals and another for central office district administrators. Both of these contain suggestions for how these individuals in their respective areas of responsibility can provide valuable assistance to you, the classroom teacher.

One danger in grantseeking that you should be aware of is that if you write many successful proposals and promote more programs than your students and school and community can assimilate, you may end up as I did: removed from the classroom, given the difficult task of helping others achieve grants success on a full-time basis, and enjoying the excitement, challenge, and rewards that the grants process brings to your school, students, colleagues, and communities.

Resource development is a very potent force in education. In fact, you may be able to effect a positive influence on more students than just those in your classroom by using your skills, this primer, and your successful example to help others find and win grants. Although I developed my grant-winning techniques over a span of twenty years, I started with my classroom. Then I was asked to help my colleagues, then my district, and finally an entire intermediate district. I know these techniques work, but only you control the real key to your grants success: your desire to bring about positive change in the classroom.

Bauer Associates supplies several valuable products and services created to support your grantseeking efforts. For a price list of our ancillary material, or to discuss the possibility of having David Bauer conduct a grants training seminar for your school or district, phone 1-800-836-0732 or visit our website at http://www.dgbauer.com.

Acknowledgments

THE INDIVIDUALS truly responsible for the creation of this book are those teachers who worked so hard to take a rebellious and troublesome youth and instill in him a love for teaching. I dedicate this book to the teachers in New York Mills Public High School who did not throw me out of class but allowed me to assist them in teaching parts of the curriculum to elementary and junior high school students. They creatively channeled my interests and energy—the same energy that could easily have been used to create chaos in the classroom.

I also acknowledge with gratitude the encouragement and hard work of my partner and associate, Donna Macrini Bauer. My early teachers and my wife helped me become a better teacher and writer than I would or could have become on my own.

The Author

DAVID G. BAUER, one of the most highly sought after speakers on grantseeking, is president of David G. Bauer Associates, Inc., a consulting firm created in 1981 to provide educationally based grantseeking and fund-raising seminars and materials. In addition, he has recently served as the Director of Development for the Center for Educational Accountability and Associate Professor at the University of Alabama at Burmingham School of Education. He has also been the Director for Extramural Funding and Grants Management at the University of Rochester School of Medicine, Department of Pediatrics, and Assistant to the President of the State University of New York College of Technology. Bauer, an acknowledged grants expert and lively lecturer, has taught more than 25,000 individuals successful grantseeking and fund-raising techniques.

Mr. Bauer is the author of *The How To Grants Manual, The Complete Grants Sourcebook for Higher Education, Administering Grants, Contracts and Funds, Successful Grants Program Management, The Fund Raising Primer, The Educator's Internet Funding Guide,* and *The Principal's Guide to Winning Grants.* He is also the coauthor of *The Complete Grants Sourcebook for Nursing and Health.* In addition, he is the developer of three videotape series—*Winning Grants 2, How To Teach Grantseeking to Others,* and *Strategic Fund Raising*—and two software programs—*Winning Links* and *Grant Winner.*

Chapter 1

Demystifying the Grants Process

WHY DO TEACHERS become involved in grantseeking? It is not in their job description, and in many cases their efforts may earn them no money. So why get involved? For more than twenty years I have asked myself and thousands of educators from elementary through postgraduate levels this very question. The answers fall into three major categories. Educators write grant proposals to try to do the following:

1. Improve teaching by changing or supplementing the curriculum, obtaining new materials, and acquiring equipment by means other than district-supported funds

2. Improve the school-community educational support system by increasing parent and volunteer participation and further involving the community in the education of youth

3. Obtain the self-esteem that comes with managing a funded project by controlling a budget, knowing that you make a difference, and asking and answering questions about education and thus expanding the universe of knowledge about how students learn

You do not need a doctorate in education or to be a statistical wizard or evaluation design genius to become involved in grantseeking. Armed with interest in education, your classroom and students, motivation, and the step-by-step techniques outlined in this book, you *can* attract grant money. Many educators would write grants for the benefits just described, but you can also earn extra pay for working on your grant-funded program. You can receive funding for extra work during school vacations, and even be released from all or part of your teaching assignment to carry out the activities described in your proposal.

In my case, I was a health teacher whose students needed information and skills to help them deal with their problems. One of my first funded projects was to develop a program to improve nutritional choices for elementary school children. I was compensated for my summer curriculum work and for the teacher in-service education I carried out. After the project was completed, I was invited to present my results at a national conference, with travel expenses provided by the grant. Not only was my program a success but I also had the enjoyment of traveling, gaining recognition from my peers, and building my feelings of self-worth. All this can be yours too when you succeed at grantseeking!

Demystifying the Grants Process

Many classroom leaders do not become involved in grantseeking because they think the process is a mystery or that it requires a support staff of professionals and a tremendous investment of time. Neither could be further from the truth. A school grants coordinator can play a supportive role in grantseeking, but you, the educator, drive the system. If you desire the resources that grantseeking can provide, your initiative and the techniques outlined in this book will guide you to grants success. As your administration seeks to replicate your success, your district will supplement the existing grants system or begin to develop one. But don't wait for the school administrator to act first. You can start now!

This book is one of three in the Jossey-Bass/Bauer Grants Series. The other two are *The Principal's Guide to Winning Grants* and *Successful Grants Program Management*. Developed for principals and district administrators respectively, both guides reaffirm their teacher's importance in developing a grants effort. Remember, you cannot be replaced in the process. You are the generator of ideas, the initiator, and the implementor. It all starts with you and takes place in your classroom and community.

Although most school systems have a central grants office that prepares and often coordinates or administers grants, it traditionally focuses on laying the groundwork for the district's federal and state grants efforts. These, usually known as Title Grants, refer to the entitlement programs that fall under the federal government's Elementary and Secondary School Act. In many cases, the types of innovations allowed under these programs are limited, and the guidelines are quite specific. However, your input into these proposals may be an avenue that you should explore with your central office personnel. By making an effort to understand your grants system you may also get help with budget development, locating potential funding sources, proposal requirements, sign-off procedures, and other formalities that could slow you up when it comes time to submit your proposal. Check with your district's grants office first. But regardless of your district's support, this book will take you beyond the grants that are based on entitlements and formulas to the billions of dollars in grants that are available for proposals that *you* write for innovative programs (projects, equipment, and so on) for *your* classroom.

Obviously you want to avoid the common pitfalls of the rejected grantseeker, increase your chances of success, and use the time you invest in grantseeking to its fullest. If you ask a foundation or corporate funding source to name the most common and fatal mistakes grantseekers make, they list many of the same problems they would have listed twenty years ago. Every year they receive piles of poorly prepared, hastily written proposals. How can you capitalize on this history of errors to develop a successful proposal? Learn what the most common mistakes are and review *Bauer's Rules of Proposal Development.*

Rule 1: A successful grants system takes work. A large percentage of the twenty thousand individuals I have instructed in my grants seminars received one grant before attending. Indeed, often their successful grant resulted from their first attempt at proposal development. But then they received a number of rejections. They came to my seminar to learn why. Basically, it's because they were just lucky the first time. As in other professions, homework, hard work, and practice are the keys to consistent grants success, not luck. (No one knows better the benefits of doing homework than we who assign it.) This primer will provide you with shortcuts, tips, and time-saving grants strategies, but you must add the work that will turn them into a successful system.

Rule 2: Funders don't care what you need or want to do. Be it curricular reform or new computer equipment, no funding source cares what you want in exactly the same way you do or sees the same results or benefits in your project as you. Grantors have their own reasons for funding projects: they fund recipients because they see or think they see benefits or results that they value. First-time recipients especially may not even be aware of grantors' reasons for funding them or of the funding sources' expectations. The message here is that if you do not have a clear picture of the benefits that your grantor expects, you may highlight the wrong data in your needs assessment. Even if you are funded, by not knowing the grantor's expectations you may provide inappropriate examples in your reporting and evaluation. This could lead to difficulty in obtaining subsequent funding.

Rule 3: Better to send your proposal to one funding source and be awarded than to a hundred and be rejected. This rule has several components.

For one, the "shotgun" approach to grantseeking repulses grantors. Just as you dislike junk mail addressed to occupant, most funders dislike receiving a proposal that has been submitted to several others. This is like haphazard bird hunting—shooting enough bullets and hoping that an unsuspecting and unlucky bird will eventually fly into one's path. However, funding sources are much smarter than birds, and this type of grantseeking insults most of them. A direct-mail appeal may motivate some individuals to make donations, but there is a great difference between $20 from one person and $20,000 from a grant award. Grant funders expect a tailored and individualized appeal that acknowledges their value to the field of education and to children.

Furthermore, rejection means negative positioning, and funding sources have long memories. In marketing terms, the positive name recognition of your school is its "positioning value," and in the grants arena you do not get credit for trying and failing.

A 1 percent success rate means that ninety-nine out of a hundred reject your proposal and have solid evidence that you do not do your homework. For example, your proposal may indicate to them that you do not know what types of projects they fund, their average grant size, or the types of institutions or organizations that they prefer to fund. Funding sources want to work with winners. You should aim at a grants success rate of 50 percent. To succeed that often, *do your homework!* Know which funders to go to, why they would want to fund you, and for what projects and amount of money.

Rule 4: Who you know is more important than what you know. As a classroom teacher, I thought that you needed to be a superintendent of schools or a politician to need to keep track of whom you knew who could influence the outcome of a grants competition. Since then, I have learned that whom you know *can* influence the outcome of a grants competition and that individuals tend to know far more people than they think. Whom you know and whom the people that you know can get in touch with are worth their weight in gold.

One of my students was the nephew of the mayor of the city I taught in. Although not a major metropolis, with eighty thousand residents it had mayoral advisory committees and funding for grants in literacy, vocational education, substance abuse, and a variety of other areas. Thanks to a common bond between me and the mayor (his nephew, my student), I was named to several of the mayor's committees and helped these groups see the wisdom of funding public elementary and junior high school educational programs to prevent problems.

In short, you must get involved and keep track of who could help you get corporate, foundation, and government grants. (More on this to come.)

Rule 5: Quality proposals do not float to the top like cream on milk—they are pushed there. After you read this book and understand how funding sources view the world and how few staff they have to help them separate the excellent proposals from the good ones, you will feel justified in using every possible advantage to ensure that your proposal gets the attention it and your students deserve.

If your proposal is worth writing, it is worth the support of all sources sympathetic to your educational cause. The more local the funding source, particularly if it is a foundation or corporation, the more likely that a local friend of the school district can influence the decision. But you must ask that friend to help you, and to do that you must keep track of your linkages to grantors.

Rule 6: Ask for the amount of money you need to complete the project, or for the portion that the grantor is likely to fund based on its granting history and pattern. Your research (homework) will tell you the funder's interests and level of support for education. If your project requires more funding than the grantor usually gives, identify the other funders you intend to approach and report any funds you have already acquired.

A proposal is not a shopping list. You should not give the funding source a choice of projects or a range of contributions. "Ask and ye shall receive" is a basic tenet of grantseeking. Give the funder a clear description of your project and specify the amount you expect from it. This will keep you from falling prey to the "dear occupant, please send money" approach that often results in a check for $100 when you wanted $10,000.

Where to Begin?

Most grantseekers are so focused on what they want to do and why that they forget to take into consideration the reasons a funding source would be interested in supporting their projects, programs, and so on. This is the old "you can't see the forest for the trees" syndrome.

Many grantseekers begin by focusing on who has money. They then try to develop a proposal that will appeal to the funding source, whether it be federal, state, foundation, or corporate. Frequently they are enticed into the grants process when they learn of the availability of grant funds through a colleague, a district publication, a professional journal, or a newsletter. Unfortunately, this sequence of events sets in motion a *reactive* grants system that is deadline driven. A reactive grants system often results in undue stress and tension, hastily prepared proposals, and usually rejection.

Do not fall into the trap. Most funding sources have been making grants for years and follow time frames that remain relatively consistent year after year. There are few surprises in the grants field, except for the number of grantees who do not learn from their fellow grantseekers' mistakes. Unless the funding source is new and has never published deadlines or made awards, there is no excuse for not doing your homework and using public records to uncover as much information as possible about the funder.

To determine how to get started in grantseeking, you must first decide to be a proactive grantseeker, first by recognizing the needs of your students and then by developing ideas, projects, and solutions to meet those needs. Armed with solutions, you *then* search for a source to fund them. When you develop a program, project, or idea that benefits your school or community and students and then seek out a funder, you establish two important concepts in the mind of a potential grantor.

Needs-Based Projects and Programs

The first concept is that your motivation to come up with an idea or solution is not that a funding source has a program deadline. Rather it is that you have assessed a situation, discovered a need, and are determined to develop a solution. In a proactive grants system you might, for example, need to provide a prospective funder with the minutes of school-community or school advisory committee meetings at which the problem was discussed and innovative ways to solve it were brainstormed months before you learned of this granting program. Unfortunately, I have worked for school districts that attempted to invent minutes from such meetings to satisfy the funder's requests for a documented concern about a problem. Just remember that your school's credibility is at stake here.

When funding sources ask to see minutes proving your efforts to develop solutions to a problem, they really want to be sure that you identified the problem before they announced having money to deal with it, and that parents, teachers, and students were involved in developing solutions to the problem.

Affordable Programs That Meet Funder Needs

The second concept you want to instill in prospective funders is that your grants system provides a program that allows them to meet their needs at a price they can afford. Most prospective grantees become consumed by their projects and are unwilling to view the projects and their benefits from the funding source's point of view. By choosing a funder according to its values, motives, and needs, you will develop a convincing proposal that demonstrates your knowledge of what the grantor funds and why. In the process, you convince the funder that it is not simply one of many you are approaching, that it has been selected as the best possible partner in creating educational change for your students.

Funding sources do not want to feel that you are throwing proposals at every possible grantor. They want to know that you target your prospects and aim for the funder that would benefit the most from making a grant to your school. Funders want to feel special—much more likely if they know you *selected* them to work with you because of the match between your program's goals and their values and expectations rather than simply because you reacted to their announcement of a deadline.

A successful grants strategy is based on proactive grantseeking. If, for example, you have determined that your students could benefit educationally from computer-assisted technology, you would not shotgun the same proposal to numerous funding sources, beg and plead with the potential grantor, and focus on your need for equipment.

Instead, you would look at the need from the funding source's point of view. Funding sources are concerned about issues such as these:

- How many students you will be able to influence over the usable life of the equipment

- What the students will be able to do that they cannot do now

- How your educational program will be adapted to integrate the use of their equipment

- How the equipment and program will be demonstrated to other teachers

- What, if any, parts of your program are innovative or different

- Whether you could present your program at a professional meeting

- Whether you could publish or submit a description of the results of your program to an educational newsletter or journal

The techniques presented in this book provide you with lifelong grantseeking skills that you can use again and again. Whether you are seeking grants for preschool, after-school programs, or community and parent education, with the help of this book, you *will* find them.

Chapter 2

Getting Ready to Seek Grants Support

CHAPTER ONE cautions against the shotgun approach to grantseeking. This chapter outlines a successful strategy for replacing the ready-fire-aim approach with a ready-aim-fire system.

As mentioned, there are two different ways to approach proposal development—reactively and proactively.

Reactive grantseekers wait for a grantseeking opportunity to present itself, perhaps through a peer, journal or newsletter, grants coordinator, or curriculum specialist. They then attempt to develop an innovative, creative, well-organized approach to solving a problem while they are in a state of frenzied confusion. Proactive grantseekers begin with a need or problem they wish to solve through grant funding. They view problems as opportunities to interest a funder in working with them to implement solutions that will improve education.

Imagine that a funding source appeared in your classroom with a shoe box filled with money and said, "I am granting this money to your school and putting you in charge of spending it. First, however, I need to know what areas or problems the money will be used for." What would your response be? Take a few minutes to consider what you would say.

This is analogous to a friend phoning to let you know that she just won a million dollars in the lottery. She asks you to suggest some vacation spots you think she might like, adding that she wants you to come along. Would you start out by mentioning only the places *you* would like to go? Most likely you would first ask some general questions to help clarify what *she* would enjoy. For example, does she like winter or summer vacations? Would she prefer visiting a tropical island to going on an African safari? In other words, you would try to assess the needs and expectations of your traveling companion. You would definitely not focus on your lifelong dream of visiting a particular destination if your friend has no interest in that spot.

Think of a grant as an agreement to travel with the grantor on a journey that benefits the funder as well as you, your classroom, and students. Today's educational needs provide many opportunities to work with funding sources. In order to determine the projects you will pursue, outline your opportunities in advance.

This does not mean writing down all solutions to education's challenges. Instead, begin by brainstorming, either by yourself or with a grants advisory committee (see Chapter Three), a list of problems or opportunities that you *may* want to deal with. This will get you going on your quest for grants.

Review your list of problems and opportunities and select one, two, or three areas for which you would like to develop solutions. By generating a list of needs (problems, areas of interest, and so on) that you would like to have an impact on, you begin to develop a proactive system based on locating funding sources that are interested in the same problems you are and therefore likely to invest in your solutions.

Create a three-ring binder (a Grants Workbook) for each need or problem area that you have identified and label the binders appropriately. Some problem areas (opportunities) will be difficult to place in one workbook because they encompass several areas of the curriculum. In this case you may want to develop one multidisciplinary book. How you do this is not as important as getting organized, selecting the problem, and getting started.

Your Grants Workbook will act as your filing cabinet. Use it to file these:

- Journal articles, studies, surveys, human interest stories, and newspaper clippings that document the problem

- Committee notes and names of other teachers and parents who are interested in collaborating on solutions to the problem

- Details of solutions to each problem

- Pertinent information on potential funding sources, including notes on your contact with them and ways to tailor your proposal to fit their needs and values

- Letters of endorsement, consortium agreements, subcontracts, and so on.

I have found that the most effective grantseeking aids are usually simple and easy to implement. For instance, by organizing a Grants Workbook for each area you are interested in, you save hours of time when you actually begin to write your proposals. In addition, a Grants

Workbook makes a positive impression on grants advisory committee members, school staff, and especially funding sources. You can order a set of dividers for your workbook to help you organize the major steps of grantseeking. These dividers or tabs can be ordered from David G. Bauer Associates, Inc.

Setting Goals

What do you expect from the grants process, and what are you willing to invest in grantseeking?

Set your sights on developing two proposals for the areas of need you have identified. Follow the system outlined in this book; depending on the area and how much grant money there is you are likely to have a 50 percent success rate. This prediction is based on the assumptions that you will not submit funding proposals that do not value your area of interest or solutions and that you will work proactively.

The following is a list of goals that will help you win grant funds.

1. Set your sights on developing a predetermined number of solutions to the problem.

2. Develop a Grants Workbook.

3. Organize a grants advisory committee or group (see Chapter Three).

4. Target a specific number of funding sources to research. Approach the potential funders by phone, personal visit, or both.

5. Write a predetermined number of proposals as a result of your contact with the potential funding sources.

One to two hours per week is a reasonable amount of time to invest in the grants process and expect to see results. Organizing your grants effort and setting goals may require you to employ some time-management techniques and do some rearranging of your daily or weekly schedule. A slight change in your routine may allow you to avail yourself, your school, and your students of the benefits that grantseeking can provide. Successful grantseeking begins with you!

Chapter 3

Forming a Grants Advisory Group

IT HAS BEEN SAID that nothing is more powerful than an idea whose time has come. To a grantor, nothing is more compelling than a proposal that involves the community. I have been employed in school districts as a health education coordinator and a community education coordinator, and as both I learned the positive value of involving the community in the grants process by initiating a grants advisory committee. The advantages of having volunteers legitimize your proposals are tremendous.

The Grants Advisory Group

In Chapter Two you were encouraged to initiate a proactive grantseeking process by selecting the problems or areas you want to address. The next step is to invite targeted individuals to attend a meeting of your grants advisory committee focused on the problem area identified. You may decide to drop the word "grants" and place more focus on the problem (for example, committee to improve fourth-grade reading). Or you may want to call it a grants advisory "group," as the word "committee" sometimes strikes fear in people's hearts. You may also choose to identify the grants group with one particular problem or opportunity. This will reduce confusion if you implement other grants advisory groups to attack other problem areas.

Before organizing any such group, check with your principal and the coordinator of any district policies, concerns, and available assistance. Once it has been formed, try to keep the group focused, manageable, and relaxed. (*Group* connotes an informal relationship where one can come and go without a membership vote, and so on.)

One important result of a grants advisory group is community involvement and empowerment. But first, the group must understand the problem. The first meeting should be informative and aimed at setting goals for action. Use some of the information provided in Chapter Six to develop the group's knowledge about the grants marketplace. This information will enthuse the members about developing solutions to the problem.

To get them started, encourage the group to react to any solutions that you may offer (to build on them, change them, react, and the like). Also encourage the members to brainstorm their own solutions and projects. The group needs to develop ownership and to buy into the needs and solutions. It is critical to your grants success to inform the members of the effect that contacting funding sources has on the positive outcome of the grants process. Studies have demonstrated a 300 to 500 percent increase in the success rate of proposals when the funding sources are contacted informally *before* the proposals are written. This entails contact well in advance of any deadline.

Your group members need to know that they play an integral role in grantseeking. Although only one person writes the proposal (usually you), all group members play a vital role in the grants process. Their most important function is to share any links they have to potential funding sources. Their initial response is likely to be that they do not know anyone who could help in the process, but a little digging will probably uncover contacts they didn't realize they had.

There are several techniques for bringing your group members to a level of commitment that assures that they will share their contacts and resources. Remember, the underlying reason for the volunteer to become involved in the first place is his or her desire to seek solutions, reduce a problem, or make educational advances for students all over the nation and in your school or classroom in particular.

The Worksheet for Planning a Grants Advisory Group (Exhibit 3.1) and Grants Resources Inventory Worksheet (Exhibit 3.2) will help you organize your grantseeking effort and guide you in involving volunteers in the process.

Planning and Initiating a Grants Advisory Group

Once you have selected the area or need the group will focus on, you are ready to consider who could provide the assistance you need in developing preproposal contact and implementing a proactive grants plan. Use the Worksheet for Planning a Grants Advisory Group (Exhibit 3.1) to help you.

Your choice of group members is very important. Do not put people on your grants advisory group solely because they are concerned and motivated. You need to have group members who can contact grant decision makers.

Exhibit 3.1

WORKSHEET FOR PLANNING A GRANTS ADVISORY GROUP

Review the suggested categories of individuals to include and write down names.

Whom to Invite

_____ Parents
_____ Corporate Leaders
_____ Foundation Board Members
_____ College Professors/Educators
_____ Retired Teachers
_____ Wealthy/Influential People
_____ Others (Please Add)

Review the Skills/Resources Needed list below and write the boldface resource description next to the possible committee members you have listed above. Avoid inviting volunteers who are overzealous about children but have no resources or contacts.

Skills/Resources Needed

- **Commitment** to children and education
- **Contacts** with people on foundation/corporate boards
- **Travel** to areas of the state/nation where there are more funders
- Willingness to share **telephone credit card** for grant-related calls
- **Marketing/sales skills**
- **Budgeting** and financial analysis skills
- Access to equipment and materials necessary to produce **audiovisual** aids depicting need
- Other

Your group should be composed of a mix of the seven categories listed on the worksheet (parents, corporate leaders, foundation board members, college professors and educators, retired teachers, wealthy and influential people, and other). The best choices within each category depend on the skills and resources needed. One technique that works well is to invite a few key individuals to help you develop a list of potential group members.

Inventory of Linkages and Resources

One of the most fascinating aspects of your grants advisory group will be the wealth of resources you uncover that have never been utilized for education. Some grantseekers are aware that a local family foundation board member on a committee may translate into a grant from that foundation, but few are aware of the resources that can be tapped in each volunteer's extended family of relatives, friends, and acquaintances.

Exhibit 3.2

GRANTS RESOURCES INVENTORY WORKSHEET

Please put a check mark next to any resource area in which you can help. Use the section at the end of the worksheet to briefly describe the resources you could provide. If you are willing to contact funding sources, please list the areas of the United States that you visit frequently.

Resource Area

_____ Evaluation of Projects

_____ Computer Programming

_____ Computer Equipment

_____ Printing

_____ Layout and Design Work

_____ Budget Skills, Accounting, Developing Cash Flow, Auditing

_____ Purchasing Assistance

_____ Audiovisual Assistance (equipment, videotaping, etc.)

_____ Travel

_____ Long Distance Telephone Calls

_____ Searching for Funding Sources

_____ Sales Skills

_____ Writing Skills/Editing Skills

_____ Other Equipment/Materials

_____ Other

Description of Resources: _____

Areas Frequently Visited: _____

You will be amazed to discover whom your advocates know—contacts you never thought you could touch. Touch is the correct word, even at the risk of sounding like a telephone company, for the billions granted by foundations and corporations are made *by* people *to* people. If the grantor knows you or knows about your program or classroom through a common linkage or friend, your proposal will get pushed to the top of the pile. One of the first lessons you should teach your grants advisory group is that just because a proposal is superbly written does not guarantee it will be funded. First it has to be read!

Don't get nervous. I am not suggesting that you abandon teaching to become a grantseeking guru, just that the more volunteers you involve in the excitement of brainstorming solutions and projects, the more linkages they will share and the more work they will do for your students.

It is critical to emphasize at this juncture that making preproposal contact with a funding source is the most important strategy that a grantseeker can employ. When volunteers and advocates are armed with the proper information, they can play a valuable role in making preproposal contact.

Volunteers and advocates give your project even more credibility than you do. Yes, you are the initiator, the implementer, the expert, and the author of the proposal, but you also receive the prestige accompanying a funded proposal, the money to spend, and the challenge of running the project. Volunteers do not receive the same benefits. Indeed, they often take time from their own children, jobs, and hobbies to work toward a greater good for all the students in your classroom and school. Also, the more your advocates and volunteers take part in the grants process, the less work you will have to do. Your role will be that of a team leader who coordinates the work of others.

What you need is an inventory of the linkages and resources of your volunteers and advocates and a way of reminding them that their relatives, friends, and acquaintances can, or know people who can, get you an appointment with a funding official. Although there are vast differences in the accessibility of the various types of funders, a linkage makes a big difference in getting an appointment even when a paid bureaucrat is in charge of the grant you are pursuing.

It is particularly difficult to get an appointment with a foundation official, mainly because fewer than a thousand of the over forty thousand foundations have offices, and there are only three thousand to four thousand foundation employees in total. In addition, most corporations prefer to have their employees volunteer at the nonprofit organizations they make grants to; some corporate grant applications ask potential grantees to list company employees who serve on the applicant's board, or even to list employees who volunteer at your school.

I suggest you have at least one meeting with your grants advisory group to stimulate their interest in solving the problem, brainstorm solutions, and foster trust and communication. Once that has been accomplished, make the group members aware of the facts about preproposal contact. After reading Chapter Six on the grants marketplace and Chapter Seven on researching potential funders, you will be able to provide your grants advisory group members with a list of potential grantors and the names of their program personnel and board members. Ask your group members to review the list and provide you with any links they have to the grantors. Encourage them to think of indirect as well as direct connections. Your group members may know someone who knows the grantor or belongs to the same club or community service organization.

Another valuable source of support your group members can provide to your grants quest are their personal resources. Distribute the Grants Resources Inventory Worksheet (Exhibit 3.2). Ask your group members to designate the types of assistance they would be willing to provide to your grants effort.

Bauer and Ferguson have developed a user-friendly software package that provides a way for you to organize and manage your linkages so that you always know who has the ability to get your foot in the door with a particular funding source. The program, *Winning Links,* operates on an IBM or IBM-compatible in either the 5.25" or 3.5" format. If you are interested in obtaining more information about this webbing and linkages software program, call 1-800-836-0732.

The more your volunteers understand the proactive grantseeking process, the more they will want to be involved in it. While the reactive approach makes grantseeking seem like a frenzied, chaotic, last-minute ordeal, proactive grantseeking is an exciting and productive mechanism for developing resources.

In an efficient grants system, the correct use of the skills, linkages, and brainpower of volunteers will reap benefits for your school time and time again. Volunteers do not want to address envelopes and lick stamps. They want to be a part of the funding equation. They want to be catalysts for *change!*

Chapter 4

Creating a Compelling Needs Statement

THE FIRST THREE CHAPTERS are based on the assumption that there are a lot of grant funds out there and volunteers to help you. You have been cautioned to avoid the major pitfalls of grantseeking (shotgunning the same proposal to several funders and last-minute reactive grantseeking) and introduced to the concept of viewing the needs of your school and community, classroom, and students from the funding source's point of view. Remember the No-Know Rule: NO funder cares what you want, you must KNOW what the funder wants. Funding sources are concerned about what *they* want and what *they* need. It is true that each year government funding sources must expend all of their grant funds and that foundations must expend at least 5 percent of the value of their assets, but they are not at a loss for potential grantees. Corporate grantors can choose how many grants they make. Many corporations choose to donate a percentage of their profits each year to nonprofit organizations, but they are not required to; they award support to the proposals that appear to promote the programs *they* value in the areas of need *they* care about. Therefore, it is imperative to learn as much as you can about how a potential funding source views the need or opportunity that your proposal will address.

Many grantseekers forget to ask themselves a critical question: Who cares?

- Who cares if the problem is reduced or solved?

- Who cares about our students and their education?

- Who cares if our curriculum is improved?

- Who cares if we promote new skills?

Asking these questions early in the grantseeking process avoids frustration, rejection, and a lot of wasted time. Remember, you are going to approach a funder requesting support to help solve a problem you feel is so important that you have already dedicated your time and resources to developing solutions.

There are two excellent reasons why you should ask yourself and your grants advisory group who would care if you complete your project, buy your equipment, or continue or expand your program. First, the answer helps you decide when it is time to abandon grantseeking as a plausible tool. Second, it helps you identify the funding sources that will be the most responsive to and interested in your project.

It is important that you know when to quit. The grants process may not provide you with the results you expect or desire. If only a few funders in your geographic area care about or value the outcome of your project, you have to alter the project significantly or give it up. This advice may appear negative or defeatist, especially coming from an author and grantseeker known for his motivational speeches, persistence, and positive attitude. It is true that I rarely give up. But if there aren't enough potential funding sources that are concerned about the need for your project, you may have to change or abandon it. You may believe that the problem is so pressing that you have to respond to it, but this can take you astray. Many grantseekers are so emotionally involved in their projects that they move directly to the solution without addressing the need. That narrows your focus and concentrates on what you want to do instead of the need and who cares about it.

Grantseekers with a narrow focus and a great deal of conviction (some are almost possessed) believe that they can get their project funded if only they can get to the funder in person and convince them to value the change the project will bring about. Listen to someone who has spent a lifetime trying to instill health-related values in children and adults: your zeal, persistence, and other positive personal characteristics cannot change another person's values. The fact is that most corporate and foundation funders do not even read proposals that do not interest or appeal to them.

So what can you do to increase your grants success? The successful grants system includes the following five steps.

1. Develop and document the need or problem (opportunity).

2. Propose several solutions.

3. Identify, through research, possible grantors that may be responsive to and interested in your project.

4. Contact the grantor (directly or through a linkage) to gather information that will help you choose the solution that is most appealing to the potential funding source.

5. Write the proposal.

Following these steps *in order* is critical. Many grantseekers believe that the project they want to get funded is so important, interesting, and creative that they skip the first four steps and begin by writing their proposal. Then they practice reactive grantseeking or spend a few minutes searching on a computer for funders before setting out to hunt grants with their shotguns.

The basics for gathering data on the need for any project or solution are founded on the principle that individuals see and hear what *they* want in a proposal. To help you understand this process, I have developed the Values Approach to Grantseeking. Each of us, including grantors, develops a set of values that guides us through our lives. This internal guidance system is based on a variety of influences, including culture, religion, family, friends, education, and so on.

The values we develop define our reality and, once formed, provide the basis for what we believe to be true (not necessarily what *is* true, but what we *believe* to be true). When we are presented with facts, proposals, and situations, we attend to what is consistent with our beliefs.

Think of these values as a pair of prescription glasses. Each of us has a distinct and different pair, and therefore we view the world differently. And the glasses have a pair of prescription hearing aids attached to them. The lenses and the hearing aids act as filters to help us attend to and store information that matches our prescription and reinforces what we believe. In essence, we each hear and see what we want to and ignore what we don't value. Complementing this theory is my conviction that we are all entitled to our own prescription glasses (or values) as long as we operate within our society's laws.

I know of few things that demonstrate individuals' values more than how they spend their money. Government, foundation, and corporate grantors tend to have different values. These differences are discussed in depth in Chapter Six. At this point, it is only important that you realize that you must be knowledgeable about grantors' values or run the risk of assuming that they use the same prescription lenses as you to view the world. I believe that the main problem with rejected proposals is that prospective grantees wrongly assume that funders' values are the same as their own.

The first step to grants success is to develop and document the need or problem, which can also be viewed as an opportunity. The natural tendency is to start with a solution, but this is not productive. Start with the need unless you are independently wealthy and can fund your own project. If you have not chosen your parents carefully or won the lottery, begin by gathering many types of data to document the need for any project. You must gather a variety of data because at this stage you do not know several things:

- What funders you will approach

- What they will value in your problem and solution

- What will best make them see the need and hence feel a compelling motivation to fund it

The Values Approach to Grantseeking will help you know what to present and how to present it to each particular grantor as well as what not to say to avoid a values conflict. Even when you and the grantor have many values in common, presenting the need for your project in the wrong way may repel a funding source. Funding sources make grants for their reasons, not yours.

It is imperative that you learn the Golden Rule of Grantseeking: Whoever has the gold makes the rules—and the grants.

Documenting Need

The needs section of a proposal has several different names, including needs statement, search of relevant literature, statement of the problem, and areas to be addressed.

Whatever it is called, its purpose is the same—to provide the grantor with several essentials:

- Substantiating evidence that the writer has a command of the current state of the art in his or her field and knows what is going on in his or her classroom and school and in other schools.

- Statistics, surveys, and other data that document the extent of the problem in the writer's school. This includes, but is not limited to, such items as standardized test scores to develop a clear picture of the extent of the problem.

- Case studies that give human interest to needs documentation. Studies and statistics tend to be viewed merely as numbers. Although factual, these may not convey that the proposal is really about students, children, future leaders, and workers in our society. Examples of what it is like to be part of the needs population can be very moving to some funders. The examples need to be real, but the names should be changed to protect individual identities. *Note:* Do not take all of your examples and condense them into one fictitious person. Use real cases only. For example, "Melissa's story is typical in my classroom . . ."

- Quotations from authorities in the field whose opinions may be viewed positively by a potential funder. Authorities might include local or national experts, elected officials, police, individuals who work with children, and so on.

Once you have selected and prioritized the problem areas you want to address, begin searching for needs documentation in your classroom, school, school system, and publications. (You may have to remove your values glasses to collect the variety of data necessary to document the need to someone who views the world differently from you.) Store your needs data in the appropriate section of your Grants Workbook (see Chapter Two). When you know whom you will approach with a proposal and what they value, you will role-play looking at the need through their values glasses in order to select the most compelling and motivating descriptions of the need. Ultimately you want to present a case that convinces the funder that a grant must be made now to reduce the problem you present by means of the solution you recommend.

Remember that the need is the difference or gap between what is now and what should be (see Figure 4.1). Each day that the needs gap is not addressed, the problem grows. Closing the gap reduces the problem and is the reason for the funding source to read the needs section of your proposal and ultimately to fund your solution.

Complete the Needs Worksheet (Exhibit 4.1) and Goals Worksheet (Exhibit 4.3). Filled-in samples of each (Exhibits 4.2 and 4.4) are included to guide you in developing a motivating and compelling case for your project.

Your time is valuable, and you must use it wisely to employ successful grantseeking techniques. My Values Approach to Grantseeking will pay dividends in success rates and dollars, considering the small investment of time you make now to describe the need. In addition, it will help you believe that you are presenting grantors with an opportunity to take part in a project that will meet their needs at the same time it meets education's needs and yours.

When you employ the more common approach to grantseeking (write proposal, look for any funder, send proposal), you do not get the

Figure 4.1

THE GAP

What exists now. What is real.	What could be. The goal.
What the present situation is.	The desired state of affairs,
How many students are at this stage.	the level of achievement

confidence and self-assurance that come from knowing you started from the need and then determined who would value the changes you propose. Making preproposal contact (Chapter Eight) is not difficult when your research already indicates that the potential funder is interested in and values what you want to do. Confidence comes from doing your homework. Efficient grantseeking requires the same effort we require of our students, who, facing an exam, feel more confident if they prepared for it. Your degree of comfort with your proposal is in proportion to the effort that went into preparing it.

Passing the exam is not the goal of education; likewise, getting the cash is not the goal of grantseeking. The end you desire is successfully completing the project and earning the funding source's respect.

The funding relationship is built on trust, and that starts with understanding how the funder views the need and the proposed solutions. Concern for funders' needs does not mean that you involve them in your classroom and abrogate your responsibilities as the educational decision maker. It does mean that you inspire their respect as an educator and leader in your field. The follow-up, the reporting, and the rapport you develop will result in a continuing relationship—not necessarily continued grants, but continued interest and possibly more investment when another of your projects meets that funder's needs.

Using the Needs and Goals Worksheets

Your completed worksheets will provide a clear picture of what is and what ought to be. They do not suggest ways to eliminate, close, or reduce the gap, but they clarify why the gap must be closed or reduced and what perspective on need a funder must have to be interested in *any* solution.

Many zealous grantseekers overlook the perspective of a funding source that has several, and often conflicting, interests. In such cases, slight changes in your documentation can make the need appeal to funding sources with varying geographic interests:

- Can your need be documented for a funder that has an interest only in your classroom, school, or community?

- Can you document the need on a county- or statewide basis?

- What is the national need to address this problem?

- Does the need exist internationally?

If you ask these questions while developing the need, you will be ready for the possible international grantor that has a facility in your community and another in Munich. Corporate funding officials may be interested in funding a project that develops math and science skills using the same conceptual solution in two different schools in two different sites—your community and Munich. Naturally, the solution you develop to reduce the problem must correlate with the need you document.

Remember to consider the need from local, regional, state, national, and international perspectives, whichever may apply.

Completing the Needs Worksheet

Refer to Exhibit 4.1. State the problem or area that your grantseeking is intended to address. Write the data that document the problem's existence in the column titled "What Exists Now—The Present State of Affairs." Record the source of the data, including the date, on the right side of the worksheet in the column titled "Source of Data." In the sample shown in Exhibit 4.2, the solutions deal with strategies to involve parents in their children's formal education and to make them aware of the influences that compete for a child's attention (television, for example).

Everyone in your grants advisory group may agree that the problem you specify on the Needs Worksheet is indeed a problem, but it must be backed up by evidence, not opinion. You can include the opinion of an expert (for example, that of the president of the PTA) as one form of documentation, but it will help only when it substantiates the facts.

Exhibit 4.1

NEEDS WORKSHEET

Completing this worksheet will help you step back from possible solutions and projects and establish that there is a gap between what is now and what should be.

Problem Area: _____

_____

_____

Documentation of the Need to Address This Problem:

What Exists Now	**Source of Data**
The Present State of Affairs	
(Studies, Facts, Surveys, Case Studies, etc.)	(Organization)
	(Journal, Newsletter, Newspaper, etc.)
	(Date of Publication)

Note: *Consider performing a survey of your classroom, school, and/or community to document that the problem exists.*

Exhibit 4.2

NEEDS WORKSHEET Sample

Completing this worksheet will help you step back from possible solutions and projects and establish that there is a gap between what is now and what should be.

Problem Area: Parents' lack of involvement in their children's formal education and lack of support for constructive informal educational experiences.

Documentation of the Need to Address This Problem:

What Exists Now—
The Present State of Affairs

4 out of 5 parents reported that they regularly discuss schoolwork with their children. Yet two-thirds of the children said their parents rarely or never talked about school with them.

Two-thirds of the parents claimed to place limits on television viewing. Two-thirds of the children said they had no limits on television viewing.

The middle school group (8th graders) reported watching 21.4 hours of television per week, in comparison to spending 5.6 hours per week on homework.

50 percent of the parents reported attending school meetings, but less than one-third had ever visited their child's classroom.

66 percent had never talked to school officials concerning their child's homework.

Source of Data

Department of Education, Office of Educational Research and Improvement, Study reported in the *Wall Street Journal* on January 3, 1992. 25,000 middle school children surveyed.

Note: *You could include findings from surveys of your classroom, school, or community; a consortium of classes; or a comparison to a classroom in Europe or another part of the world.*

Most successful grantseekers list the problem indicators first when they document the need, because the indicators help individuals motivate themselves to make a difference and do something about the problem.

Complete the Needs Worksheet, but try to hold yourself and your volunteers back from moving quickly to solutions. You may find it helpful to have your grants advisory group review your completed worksheet and provide comments, additions, and so on. However, the best course of action would be to have a volunteer review the facts, conduct a search of the literature, and add to your base of knowledge. You will probably never use all the data you collect in any single proposal, but the more data you

Exhibit 4.3

GOALS WORKSHEET

Problem Area:_____

_____

_____

_____

_____

If the needs documented on the Needs Worksheet were fulfilled and the problem was eliminated, what would result? What is the *desired* state of affairs? The ultimate end? The answer to these questions states the goal. The Needs Worksheet documents what exists now. The Goals Worksheet documents what ought to be. The goal provides purpose, direction, and motivation for grantseeking.

Goal: _____

_____

_____

_____

_____

Record studies, quotations, and research findings that document what ought to be. Provide sources and dates.

Studies—Quotations—Research Findings   **Source—Date**

Note: *This is not the place to list solutions. Means of closing gaps are solutions; they are discussed in Chapter Five.*

have the easier it will be to tailor your proposal to the particular perspective of a grantor.

Completing the Goals Worksheet

Referring to Exhibit 4.3, describe the problem area in the space provided. You may find it helpful to provide copies of the Needs Worksheet to those completing the Goals Worksheet so that they can address the question already posed on that worksheet.

When completing the Goals Worksheet, start by asking yourself what the situation would be if the problem were solved. What would the students, school, district, parents, society be like? You are describing an ideal state of affairs. Naturally, not all children will reach their potential; we will

Exhibit 4.4

GOALS WORKSHEET Sample

Problem Area: Parents' lack of involvement in their children's formal education and lack of support for constructive informal educational experiences.

If the needs documented on the Needs Worksheet were fulfilled and the problem was eliminated, what would result? What is the *desired* state of affairs? The ultimate end? The answer to these questions states the goal. The Needs Worksheet documents what exists now. The Goals Worksheet documents what ought to be. The goal provides purpose, direction, and motivation for grantseeking.

Goal: Parents and teachers acting as responsible partners who work together to maximize children's educational achievement.

Record studies, quotations, and research findings that document what ought to be. Provide sources and dates.

Studies—Quotations—Research Findings	Source—Date
Students whose parents discussed their schoolwork recorded higher grades.	Dept. of Education Study, *Wall Street Journal* 1/3/92
Television viewing restrictions tended to boost grades.	Dept. of Education Study, *Wall Street Journal* 1/3/92
"Burden of education should not be on the teachers and schools alone." Education Department study says, "Parents have a major role to play."	Dept. of Education Study, *Wall Street Journal* 1/3/92
Home-based guidance program in Rochester schools demonstrates educational improvement in low-income students. Homeroom teacher acts as liaison between schools and parents. When teacher makes home visits, children do better in school.	Harvard University, 3-year study, Berea, OH, *Democrat & Chronicle* 11/28/91.
Preschool children from single-parent homes have better verbal skills than children from two-parent homes (more one-on-one communication).	Unpublished study 1989–90, Deidre Madden, Baldwin Wallace College, Berea, OH, *Democrat & Chronicle* 11/28/91.
Harrison, Arkansas—Students score in top 10 percent of the nation in test scores, yet Arkansas ranks 272 of 327 in education taxes. One of the lowest tax rates in the U.S. Money may not be the resource that makes the difference. Parents volunteer in their children's classrooms one hour per week. Duties include making copies, grading papers, working with students, listening to students read. Basically, the parents save teachers time. Parents and teachers meet on school councils and determine the educational goals for next year. Each school reports progress toward goals in a newspaper advertisement. School system received 10 new computers donated by civic clubs. Parents made speeches at clubs.	*USA Today* 11/18/91; study identifies good schools through "School Match" of Columbus, Ohio. "School Match" provides information to families moving to new areas.

Frank Newman, President of Education Commission, states, "They're saying parents are important and teachers are important and they should be part of running the schools."

not be able to totally eliminate prejudice or bigotry. But goals provide direction. They tell us where to aim. They are not usually measurable.

To help you legitimize and clarify your goal, use the space provided on the Goals Worksheet to list studies, quotations, and research findings that show that the direction you want to move in is justified and proper.

In the sample shown in Exhibit 4.4, the problem described is parents' lack of involvement in their children's education. This problem has yielded a goal statement that answers the question "What if the problem were solved?" In this ideal state of affairs, parents and teachers would act as responsible partners and work together to maximize the educational achievement of children.

The next step is to brainstorm strategies (solutions) for closing the gap you have documented.

Chapter 5

Generating Proposal Ideas

YOUR TASK NOW is to increase your success in attracting grant funds to reduce or solve the problem you documented in Chapter Four. At this point, many grantseekers believe they're ready to write their proposals. They think they have already identified the best possible solution, and they may have a deadline looming in the not-too-distant future.

But wait. Have you considered alternative solutions? To avoid the narrow, self-centered focus of many grantseekers ("I want to do this project my way"), keep in mind the Values Approach to Grantseeking, which focuses on the grantor's values.

You want to convince the grantor that you are an outcome-oriented grantseeker. It is critical that the solution you suggest will make a meaningful contribution to reducing the need and closing the gap between what is and what ought to be. Indeed, you should generate several possible ways to alleviate the problem.

Most grantseekers have only one solution (their favorite), and they want to implement it *now*. But approaching a granting source with only one solution is risky. First, you may be perceived as narrow-minded; funders prefer that you consider many alternatives and choose the best. They may even want to know why you selected one alternative over others. Second, the single solution you choose may not meet grantors' expectations. For example, they may find your problem compelling but your solution very weak. Just as you might turn off a grantor with a needs statement that is incompatible with their values, you might propose a solution that you prefer only to discover that it is not the grantor's choice.

Because a proposal gets funded does not necessarily mean it was well conceived, well written, or outstanding. Perhaps it simply presented the best solution in a specific area of the funding source's interest.

How do you develop and present the best solution to a grantor? One of the most vital steps in my Values Approach to Grantseeking is to generate alternative solutions to the problem. A well-conceived and well-thought-out solution is the bottom line in proposal generation.

What works best is to generate several potential solutions without spending a lot of time and energy on detail. The object is to make preproposal contact with the potential grantor and to try to involve it in choosing which solution to present in your proposal.

Your final grant proposal must present one solution that will have an impact on the problem and be viewed positively by the funder. Your research on the prospective funding source should yield information that will help you choose that solution. You cannot present a shopping list in your final proposal, but the greater the number of good ideas you develop the better your chance of selecting the best solution.

Learning About Previously Funded Proposals

Through your search of the literature and grantor research, you will be able to identify the schools and educational groups that have previously received funding in your problem area and what solutions they proposed. Learning about the success and failure of past grants will help you do the following:

- Know which approaches to discuss with prospective grantors
- Avoid duplicating a failed proposal
- Suggest new approaches that capitalize on the experiences of past grantees
- Inform members of your grants advisory group of what solutions have been proposed and thereby provide a basis for generating new ideas

Who Should Help You Develop and Improve Proposal Ideas

Grantors are leery of grantseekers whose solutions do not take into account the opinions of others. Grantmakers are much more sophisticated than we may want to acknowledge. They know that the best approach takes into consideration the concerns, criticisms, and improvements of many individuals. Even in cases where grantmakers do not allow any preproposal contact, they want you to consider the opinions of other experts in developing your approach. You may still say "I" in your proposal, but the sense you want to convey to the prospective grantor is that several individuals, groups, or organizations have been involved in generating, critiquing, and endorsing the chosen solution.

Here are potential partners for developing and improving your proposal ideas:

- Your grants advisory group
- Fellow educators from your school and other schools
- Administrators in your school—curriculum specialists, school coordinators, and so on
- Students—current elementary and middle school students, high school students, graduates of your system, dropouts (indicating that the current system failed)
- Parents
- Concerned community members
- College and university professors and other professionals in the field of education
- Political allies and elected officials or their administrative assistants

How to Generate Ideas

Years of experience have shown me that you do not need to hold a formal meeting of your key partners in order to develop and improve your proposal ideas. Other than during a scheduled meeting of your grants advisory group, it is best to approach your other partners in small, informal groups or individually. The most creative solutions are often arrived at over a cup of coffee or on a work break.

Nor do you need to set aside large blocks of undisturbed time to create unique solutions; most experts say that a time restriction of five to eight minutes should be observed when groups are brainstorming solutions. The following guidelines have worked for me with my grants advisory committees and small groups of selected individuals.

- Give the participants a brief description of the problem you are trying to solve. You may even decide to distribute your Needs and Goals Worksheets (Exhibits 4.1 and 4.3) to establish the gap that the solution will seek to reduce.
- Tell your participants that their goal is to generate ideas about and solutions to the stated problem.
- Set a five-minute limit for expressing ideas.
- Appoint an individual to record the suggestions.

In some cases, I include information on what solutions have already been attempted.

Using the Chapter Worksheets

Next, list the group's proposed solutions on the Worksheet for Developing Solutions and Projects to Reduce the Problem (Exhibit 5.1). Make a copy of the completed worksheet for each participant and ask each to rank the solutions, with number 1 indicating her or his favorite. This will help you analyze and evaluate the ideas.

Then ask the group to focus on their two favorite solutions. Jot them down on the Worksheet for Developing the Top Two Suggested Solutions

---

Exhibit 5.1

WORKSHEET FOR DEVELOPING SOLUTIONS AND PROJECTS TO REDUCE THE PROBLEM

Problem: _____

_____

_____

List any and all proposed solutions. No discussions, please. Discuss the ideas after the time allotted for brainstorming has expired. Then request each participant to rank order the proposed solutions, with 1 being the favorite.

Rank **Proposed Solutions/Projects to Reduce the Problem**

-
-
-
-
-
-
-
-
-
-
-
-
-
-
-
-
-
-
-
-

Exhibit 5.2

WORKSHEET FOR DEVELOPING THE TOP TWO SUGGESTED SOLUTIONS TO THE PROBLEM

Problem: _____

_____

_____

_____

Describe the top two proposed solutions briefly and give a rough estimate of the cost of each. Also provide an estimate of the cost per student or teacher. Include the number of individuals who would benefit directly from each solution and the number who could benefit indirectly through duplication of the approach at other schools. List the drawbacks of each (that is, those things that would impede its success).

Ask the following of each solution. Would you fund this idea with a grant? Will the benefits justify the money expended?

Solution #1:

Solution #2:

to the Problem (Exhibit 5.2). Discuss and record the advantages and disadvantages of each of the five solutions.

Ask the group to arrive at a rough cost estimate of each of the solutions. However, do not eliminate an approach because it seems expensive at this point. You do not have any money yet; why place cost constraints on your ideas? Encourage your participants to explore solutions of various costs that have different positive and negative points.

In the completed sample worksheet shown in Exhibit 5.3, the group ranked all proposed solutions that they had listed on a Worksheet for Developing Solutions and Projects to Reduce the Problem. They then transferred the top two solutions to the Worksheet for Developing the Top

---

Exhibit 5.3

WORKSHEET FOR DEVELOPING THE TOP TWO SUGGESTED SOLUTIONS TO THE PROBLEM Sample

Problem: Parents' lack of involvement in their children's K–12 in-school education and lack of support for outside-of-school education activities such as the completion of homework.

Describe the top two proposed solutions briefly and give a rough estimate of the cost of each. Also provide an estimate of the cost per student or teacher. Include the number of individuals who would benefit directly from each solution and the number who could benefit indirectly through duplication of the approach at other schools. List the drawbacks of each (that is, those things that would impede its success).

Ask the following of each solution. Would you fund this idea with a grant? What is the extent of the benefits for the money expended?

Solution #1: Develop a parent-teacher-student education contract that outlines each party's responsibility to support education. Review and renew every month on a three-part carbonless form.
Cost: $2 per student
Benefits: Students, parents, and teachers each have a copy of the expectations

Solution #2: Provide an electronic interface (Internet access or fiber-optic cable) where parents can access their children's homework assignments and homework help, and incorporate solution #1 into this solution.

Two Suggested Solutions to the Problem. It is important to note that the two listed solutions are not mutually exclusive and that the integration of several strategies can sometimes yield an exemplary proposal for a model project.

In this example, the educator and parents advisory group decided that the most interesting combination was to involve students, parents, and teachers in developing a learning contract for each month. They decided to report to parents on student progress by means of videotapes and home and school visits.

In your situation, the process will encourage your volunteers to buy in to the solution and result in their continued support of the rest of the grants process.

Chapter 6

Understanding the Grants Marketplace

IF YOU HAVE A SPECIFIC grantor's program announcement and only one or two weeks to prepare your proposal, you do not have time to read this chapter nor take advantage of the facts and strategies suggested. This chapter is intended for proactive grantseekers who are looking for the best match between their proposal ideas and a grantor's needs. Reactive grantseekers whose rejected proposals prove they did not locate the right funder in their latest attempts at grantseeking will also find this chapter worthwhile, especially if they decide to incorporate preproposal contact into their future grantseeking attempts.

Just as teachers face a myriad of questions from well-intentioned seekers of knowledge (their students), I am asked questions by my well-intentioned students—grantseekers searching for the secret to grant funding. The two most common concerns are where to go for grant funding (in other words, which grants marketplace will provide the best opportunity? Corporations? Foundations? Government?) and which grantor within that marketplace is best for a given project.

The obvious possibility is for me to tell them the correct answers. But, as a teacher, I am not supposed to give the answers. I am supposed to help my students find them. Teachers want students to develop the concepts that will organize the students' data and lead them to discover the answers for themselves. We all know how much more difficult it is to teach the process than to give the answers.

Recently a participant at one of my grants seminars asked me to explain how I select a type of funding source and a specific grantor for a project idea. As I analyzed the process I use, I was reminded of my high school geometry teacher. (After several years in her class we came to know each other quite well.) My geometry teacher would present a problem and the postulates to use in proving the theorem. In a frenzy of confusion and with time running out, I often pleaded that I just did not know where to start. Her response was, "Well, it is obvious where to begin. Take postulate number three and . . ." But what was obvious to the specialist, my geometry teacher, was not obvious to me, the geometry student. The teacher knew the answer, the geometric concepts, and the correct approach. My approach was to try each postulate until something worked. (Unfortunately, the problem then became a permutation-combination and took ten hours to solve.) I never did pass the course, but although my failure did not have a drastic effect on my career, you and your projects are critically important to your students, to you, and to me.

Your problem is to determine where to get the money for your project. To figure this out, you need to develop your knowledge of the general types of funding sources and their major differences and similarities. The Grantseekers' Decision Matrix (Table 6.1) will help you develop the insights you need to find the funder best suited to your school and your project.

Use the matrix each time you begin the process of selecting the most appropriate grantor for your project. This system follows the Values Approach to Grantseeking developed in the previous chapters and is based on how each general type of funder views the need for the project and your qualifications. Using the matrix will give you a rough assessment of the potential interest of the various types of funders. Grantors are not easy to characterize, and there are many generalizations represented on the matrices. However, the purpose of the matrix is to provide you with a logical place to start your search for the best funder. By using it, you will be able to assess how well your school and project fit each grantor type.

Grantseekers' Decision Matrix

The matrix has the following ten columns: Type of Funder, Geographic Need, Type of Project, Award Size, School's Image, Credentials of Project Director, Preproposal Contact, Proposal Content, Review System, and Grants Administration. Let's look first at funder types. Chapter Seven provides details on how to move from the type of funder to their individual granting programs.

Column 1: Type of Funder

This column lists nine major funding sources. Together they award over $106 billion each year in grants.

Federal

The federal government provides over $85 billion in grants each year through 1,300 plus separate granting programs. To understand government grant support for elementary and middle schools, you must remember that our country's founders decreed that responsibility for any

Table 6.1

GRANTSEEKER'S DECISION MATRIX

Type of Funder	Geographic/Need	Type of Project	Grant Award Size For Field of Interest	School's Image	Credentials of P.I. or P.D.	Preproposal Content · Any Face-to-Face is +	Proposal Content	Review System	Grants Administration (Rules)
1. Federal	Varies—but must have national/ international	Model innovation Research	Large	Very national image+	National image	Write, phone, go and see	Extensive— many forms long	Staff and peer review. Human subjects & animals	Many/compiles OMB cir audits + match $
2. State	State/Local need	Model and Replication	Medium Small	Statewide image+	Statewide image	Write, phone, go and see	Extensive— many forms long	Staff and some peer review	Many/ complex audits + match $
3. National General- Purpose	National need— Local/Regional Population	Model innovation	Large Medium	National image+	National+	Write, phone	Short-concept paper then longer if interested	Staff and some peer review	Few audits and rules
4. Special-Purpose	Need in area of interest	Model innovation Research	Large to Small	Image not as critical as solution is	Image in field of interest+	Write, phone	Short-concept paper—longer form if interested	Board review (some staff)	Few audits and rules
5. Community	Local need	Operation Replication Building/Equipment	Small	Local image+	Respected locally	Write, phone, go and see	Short-letter proposal	Board review	Few audits and rules
6. Family	Varies—but geographic concern for need	Innovation Replication Building/Equipment Some research	Medium Small	Regional image+	Local/regional	Write, phone	Short-letter proposal	Board	Very few audits and rules
7. Corporate—Large	Near plants or offices	Product Development Replication Building/Equipment	Medium Small	Local image+ Employee involvement	Local, national	Write, phone, go and see	Short-letter proposal	Contributions Committee	Very few audits and rules
8. Corporate—Small	Very near to company	Same	Medium Small	Local image critical	Local	Write, phone, go and see	Short-letter proposal	Owner/Family	Very few audits and rules
9. Nonprofit Organizations and Service Clubs	Local	Replication Building/Equipment Scholarship	Small	Local image and member involvement	Local	Write, phone, present to committee or to members	Short-letter proposal	Committee review and/or member vote	Few rules and audit

functions not specified in the Constitution rests with state and local governments. The U.S. Department of Education is not responsible for educating our children. We, at the local level, are responsible.

The federal role has traditionally been to supply grant monies to initiate and, in some cases, support educational programs that affect many or all of the states. The Elementary and Secondary Schools Act funds federal involvement in state and local schools. The Department of Education defines who is eligible to receive these funds. Eligible organizations may be designated for block grant funding through state agencies, who receive the funding and redistribute it to schools, or the schools may apply directly to the federal government. Program eligibility information states are eligible recipients. School districts are designated as local educational agencies (LEAs). Programs funded by the Elementary and Secondary Schools Act are referred to as title or chapter grants. You should always check with your district superintendent's office to see if your project or idea might be covered by a title grant or state block grant. Some entitlement programs have funds for special projects. In addition, the federal contact person may advise you of other programs appropriate for your projects and ideas.

The Department of Education seeks to improve education by sponsoring grant competitions that encourage educational research and innovative approaches to education. The federal government does support continuing programs such as Head Start and Early Start, but the Education Department uses much of its funds to initiate, prove, or demonstrate what works in education. The continuation or implementation of a proven model is the responsibility of the state and local school district. Therefore, the federal government is *not* a good source to approach for continuing or reinstating a program that your district will no longer support. You will have much better results if you turn to federal funding sources for support for programs that develop innovative or creative models for change in education.

With a Department of Education budget of approximately $40 billion, the federal government should be your first choice when you are looking for support for new programs.

State

State grants programs are established and supported through either federal block grants, pass-through funding, or state tax dollars. The amount of state grant funds available varies greatly, and the projects these funds support depend on each state's educational programs and unique needs.

Many states have instrumented their own technology funding programs. In some cases federal funding may provide money to the states

(Technology Innovation, for example) while reserving a portion for a national Grants Competition for schools. Many education dollars are received by your state as a result of formulas or criteria based on needs, population, and so on. The state may pass on the money as a grant to all eligible schools using a formula or may use the grants mechanism as a means of disseminating it.

National General-Purpose Foundations

These are large, well-known foundations. Though they are only about a hundred of the total forty thousand U.S. foundations, they hold a large percentage of the $276.6 billion in foundation assets. Of the $13 billion plus in grants awarded annually by foundations, this small group contributes the most.

National general-purpose foundations employ staff and may even use experts in the field to review proposals. Most of the three thousand to four thousand individuals employed by foundations work for this small group. National general-purpose foundations fund a wide variety of interests and do so on the national and local levels, and, in some instances, internationally. They often have an interest in educational innovation and education as it relates to minorities and economic concerns. They spend a good deal of time reading proposals, meet more often than smaller foundations, and are often available for preproposal contact. Examples include the Ford Foundation and the Rockefeller Foundation.

Special-Purpose Foundations

These foundations support a relatively narrow range of grant interests. Numbering only a few hundred foundations, they still constitute a major influence in their fields of choice. They have directors and staff and, similar to large national general-purpose foundations, meet more often and spend more time reading proposals than other types of foundations. They have offices and employees, are focused on their interest area, and have experts in the field on their staff. Examples in education include the Exxon Education Foundation and the Carnegie Foundation for the Advancement of Teaching.

Community Foundations

This is the fastest-growing type of foundation in terms of number and assets. Among them, they made 25 percent more grants in the most recent reporting year (1997). Usually named after the geographic area they serve, community foundations now number more than three hundred. Most have full- or part-time staff and the composition of their boards normally reflects the community they seek to enhance. Their funds are usually generated from bequests, and their grants must benefit the community they are located in. Examples include the Cleveland Foundation, the Chicago Foundation, and the San Diego Foundation. You need to find out if there is one in your community.

Family Foundations

These account for approximately 80 percent of all foundations. However, they award less than 20 percent of all foundation grants. Only the largest of the thirty-two thousand plus family foundations have a director, and few have staff.

Family foundations normally award smaller grants and have little staff or peer review. Their boards usually meet only one or two times a year for an average length of three hours. Therefore, decisions are made quickly and without much opportunity for discussion with prospective grantees, either before or after the deadline.

To help you understand this marketplace, consider that only 78,296 grants for more than $10,000 were made in 1997. These totaled over $6.9 billion, or just over half of the $13 billion in total foundation grants. The other $6.1 billion plus was made up of hundreds of thousands of grants for less than $10,000, and most of these came from family foundations. These grants went to approximately 625,000 tax-exempt groups. Approximately 25 percent of their grants went to education, and only a portion of those went to the estimated 71,887 elementary and middle schools in the United States. The rest went to higher education.

Corporate—Large

Large corporate grants come from corporate funds and corporate foundation assets. There are approximately five million corporations in the United States and only a few thousand use a corporate foundation to make their grants. Some corporations make grants from both their contributions program and their corporate foundation. The main difference between the two is that the corporate foundation allows for a more even distribution of grants because assets can be tapped to fund a more consistent granting program when profits are low. Another big difference is that only the corporate foundation's tax return is available for public scrutiny. Therefore, controversial grants are often made through the corporation without the knowledge of the public or the corporation's stockholders.

Corporate grants totaled over $8.2 billion in 1997 and have exceeded inflation in only two of the last five years. A recent study showed that only 35 percent of corporations make tax-deductible contributions to nonprofit organizations. But of those that do, education is a primary area of interest (35 percent). Corporations are interested in how the grants they fund will affect their workers, the children of their workers, their profits, and their products. If you can interest local employees to volunteer for your project, you can increase your chances of success.

Most companies restrict their grants to organizations located close to their facilities. For those companies not located near you, consider that a grant to your classroom offers them a chance to position their products with students, teachers, and parents and provides them with an opportunity to learn how to improve their products. These large corporations normally have a contributions officer in charge of their giving programs and spend more time reading proposals than some foundations. Having a corporation's employees volunteer at your school is critical to securing the corporation's support. Examples in the large corporate category include IBM, Apple Computer, 3M, Texaco, and Kodak.

Corporate—Small

It is difficult to find accurate information on the grantors in this category, but these smaller corporations provide an excellent funding prospect for schools because they give where they live. In addition, they often have more ties to the community and its schools than other types of funding sources. The key to grants support from this group is their involvement in your school and its projects. Examples include small businesses, family businesses, and owner-operated franchises such as McDonald's, Jiffy Lube, Taco Bell, and Burger King. For example, McDonald's provides grants through its local cooperatives as well as Ronald McDonald Children's Charities national giving program.

Nonprofit Organizations and Service Clubs

This group includes professional associations, Hellenic groups, business groups, service clubs, and membership groups. Many have an education or youth subcommittee that actively seeks projects worthy of their support. A list of service clubs is usually posted on a sign as you enter a community, and the sign often lists meeting places and times. Nonprofit organizations and service clubs can be approached to support parts of a costly proposal or a matching component, or to challenge other organizations to raise an amount equal to their grant. Examples include Rotary clubs, Kiwanis clubs, African American groups, and so on.

Columns 2 Through 10

The Grantseekers' Decision Matrix can be used in many ways. Columns 2 through 10 provide information that will help you select the best type of funding source for your project. For example, if your problem and project are unique to your geographic area, you might look more closely at those funders whose primary concerns are local.

Your type of project may also be used to determine the most likely funder. For instance, is it a model project? Replication? Research? Equipment?

Another important variable related to your success is selecting the appropriate funder for your grant size or request. In other words, you wouldn't approach a small service club for full support of a project with a large grant request.

Your school's track record with grantors and who has invested in your school previously is also important, as is the image of the project director. Each type of funding source will look at the credentials of the project director differently. But name recognition and credibility are usually important to all.

Your ability to contact the prospective grantor, its proximity to you, and its expected protocols are also critical to choosing the right funder.

The required proposal content, review system used, and grants administration rules are variables that give you an indication of how much time will be required of you and your grants committee in writing and administering your grant.

For those of you who just want computers for your classroom, you can see that you are limited in your grants choices. To attract funding from most grantmakers, you must consider how you can make your proposal innovative and creative. If you want to replicate what another educator has proven successful, you are limited to community foundations and some local family foundations. Even these limited choices view computers as a means to an end; they want to know what student skills and scores will change once the computers are in use.

The next chapter helps you locate specific grantors within each type of funding source.

Chapter 7

Researching Potential Funders

YOUR ULTIMATE GOAL is to secure funding. To do this, you must develop a broad list of possible funders, eliminate the least likely prospects, and select the one most likely to support your great idea. There are many resources right in your community to help you research potential funders—so many, in fact, that the number of potential funders you uncover could actually be confusing. The key to finding the source most likely to fund you is to keep in mind the Values Approach to Grantseeking: always look at your grant idea from the point of view of the potential grantor. This means defining your project and its benefits from the grantor's viewpoint.

Computer databases and resource books are organized and indexed by subject area, geography, eligibility, and several other variables. Your success in using them depends on several things:

- Your selection of research or key search words

- The approaches or solutions you develop

- Your willingness to change or modify the solution to appeal to different types of funders

Key Search Words

Many standard grants resources have a subject-area index. Subject areas such as child welfare, early childhood education, youth, and so on can be thought of as key words. Under each category are listed all the funding sources that have expressed an interest in that area. Therefore, key words can help you search for potential funding sources, which is why they are called key search words.

Start by determining the key words that can be related to your project. Also, think of ways you could change or adapt your project to relate to more key words or subject areas. The object is not merely to relate your project or idea to as many key words as possible but also to determine the ways it could be related to various funders' interests.

For example, say you are interested in using computers to teach reading to fourth graders. A particular funder may have an interest in literacy. If you define your project as one related to literacy, that particular funder will end up on your list of possible grantors. (Remember, not all the funders speak the same language as you or have your vocabulary.)

Use the Key Words Worksheets in this chapter to help you look at your project or solution from the viewpoint of the funding source. The Key Words Worksheet for Government Grantseeking (Exhibit 7.1) lists key words or descriptors that relate to federal programs dealing with the entire field of education as well as those relating to programs dealing with elementary education only. The Key Words Worksheet for Foundation and Corporate Grantseeking (Exhibit 7.2) lists many key words found in computer-assisted retrieval systems and reference books. Review the lists and designate those words that can be related to your project.

Armed with your key words, you are ready to initiate your search for funds. As discussed next, you do not need to spend a lot on reference books or computer-based search systems. Many can be obtained inexpensively or for free. You may wish to start with a computer-assisted grants search.

Exhibit 7.1

KEY WORDS WORKSHEET FOR GOVERNMENT GRANTSEEKING

The federal government uses the following subject index in describing grant opportunities in education. Review the list and indicate the key words that relate to your project. You may find it helpful to make a brief notation of any significant ways you could change your solution to make it relate to that key word.

The following descriptors relate to federal programs dealing with the whole area of education.

Adult Education	Elementary Education	Indian Education
Disadvantaged Education	Health Education	International Education
Early Childhood Education	Humanities Education	Tools for Schools

The following descriptors relate to federal programs dealing with elementary education.

Elementary Education Arts	Handicapped	Neglected and Delinquent
Elementary Education Bilingual	Homeless Children	Physical Fitness
Chapter 1	Immigrant Children	Private Schools
Chapter 2	Impact Aid	School Dropout Prevention
Computer Learning	Math/Science	Talent Search
Disadvantaged/Deprived	Migrant Education	Technology
Drug-Free Schools	Elementary Education Minorities	Upward Bound
Gifted and Talented Students		

Exhibit 7.2

KEY WORDS WORKSHEET FOR FOUNDATION AND CORPORATE GRANTSEEKING

The following key words are used in many electronic data retrieval systems and printed reference books. Review the list and indicate the key words that relate to your project. You may find it helpful to make a brief notation of any significant changes in your solution in order to relate to that key word.

Adult/Continuing Education Programs

Alternative Modes/Nontraditional Study

Arts Education Programs

Bicultural/Bilingual Education Programs

Biological Sciences Education Programs

Business Education Programs

Career Education Programs

Children/Youth

Cognition/Information Processing

Communications Education Programs

Computer-Assisted Instruction

Computer Science Education Programs

Computer Sciences

Conference Support

Early Childhood/Preschool Education

Educational Counseling/Guidance

Educational Reform

Educational Studies—Developing Countries

Educational Testing/Measurement

Educational Values

Elementary Education

Employment Opportunity Programs

Employment/Labor Studies

Energy Education Programs

English Education Programs

Environmental Studies Education Programs

Fine Arts Education Programs

Foreign Language Education Programs

Foreign Scholars

Gifted Children

Handicapped Education Services

Handicapped Vocational Services

Handicapped/Special Education Programs

Health Education Programs

Humanities Education Programs

Illiteracy

Information Dissemination

International Studies Education Programs

Journalism Education Programs

Learning Disorders/Dyslexia

Mathematics Education Programs

Minority Education Programs

Music Education Programs

Nutrition Education Programs

Opportunities Abroad

Parental Involvement in Education Philosophy

Philosophy of Education

Physical Education Programs

Physical Sciences Education Programs

Precollegiate Education—Arts Education Programs

Precollegiate Education—Bilingual Education Programs

Precollegiate Education—Economics Education Programs

Precollegiate Education—Humanities Education Programs

Precollegiate Education—Professional Development

Precollegiate Education—Science/Math Education Programs

Prizes/Awards

Professional Development

Professional/Faculty Development

Reading Education Programs

Remedial Education

Rural Education

Rural Services

Rural Studies

Teacher Education

Telecommunications—Education Materials

Vocational/Technical Education

Women's Education Programs—Business Management

Women's Education Programs—Science/Engineering

Women's Studies Education Programs

Youth Employment Opportunity Programs

Performing a Computer-Assisted Grants Search

Check with your district's grants office to find out what computer assistance is available to you. Your school or district librarian may be able to help. Most libraries are linked to DIALOG, a database of government and private funding sources, and they may carry out a search for you at no charge.

Also, invite a college or university faculty or staff member to be part of your grants advisory group. He or she should not be required to come to the meetings but should be willing to help you locate potential funders. Most colleges have a grants office, and even very small colleges often have computer-assisted search systems, such as the Sponsored Programs Information Network (SPIN) and the Illinois Research Information System (IRIS). Be sure to inform your potential college volunteer that you already have a list of key words for searching federal programs and private grantors (foundation and corporate). This helps to ensure a positive response.

Even if your district provides search services, I recommend that you include representatives of higher education in your grants process. The connection with a college or university provides many advantages:

- Access to professional educators who have the credentials you may need to appeal to some funders

- A different perspective for brainstorming that may lead to alternative solutions and ideas you would not have generated on your own

- A possible consortium relationship or an alternative organization through which to submit your proposal

- Access to the inexpensive labor of graduate students,

- Assistance in developing evaluation designs, statistical analysis, and data manipulation

- Expertise with curriculum design

Including a representative of higher education in your group does not mean giving the project to her or him. You can maintain control over any components you wish to. Professors of education or related fields will usually be very willing to work with you because you can offer them access to your school and classroom, an opportunity to work with your students, extra income (if they work on a grant at their college, they get release time but not much extra cash compensation), and contact with elementary, middle, and junior high school teachers.

For these reasons (plus their love for the field of education) you should be able to involve these fellow professionals in your project and get research into funding sources done on their computer database.

You can gain access to the federal government's grants database (the *Catalog of Federal Domestic Assistance*) through the Internet. To get there, go to Gopher to: portfolio.standard.edu:1970/1100334 or solar.rtd.utk. edu/11/federal/CFDA. The Department of Education's website is http://gcs.ed.gov/

The Foundation Center has a CD-ROM database that is available at many of its cooperating collections; see the list in Exhibit 7.4. Call your closest cooperating collection for availability and usage rules.

Government Grant Information Sources

Federal and state grants come from tax dollars and are therefore subject to many rules and to the Freedom of Information Act. This means that you have a right to free or inexpensive access to all information on federal grant opportunities. You should have a basic knowledge of the federal grants system even if your college advisory group member arranges a free search for you.

Government grant opportunities for education are available to your school either directly from federal programs or indirectly from federal programs passed through states. Some states develop their own grants programs, but there is no uniform mechanism for inviting applications for these funds. It is your responsibility to alert your building principal and district grants people of your interest in state grant opportunities. Because few states have grants systems as organized as the federal government's, you may find it helpful to check directly with your state education department, which can place you on its mailing list for information on programs, advise you of websites, and e-mail alerts to you.

Direct federal grant opportunities are a different story. As all prospective grantees must have an equal opportunity to learn about and apply for federal funds, there is a special system for the dissemination of federal grant information.

Ask educators in schools what they think of when they hear the words "federal grant opportunity." Chances are they will describe scenes of confusion and panic. The reason is that for many school districts, meeting a federal grants deadline means last-minute, chaotic scrambling—a result of reactive grantseeking. But educators can develop successful federal proposals and deal effectively with the pressure of deadlines by being knowledgeable about the federal grants process. I have been a consultant to several school districts seeking to develop an improved and proactive federal grants system. These districts now plot federal deadlines a year in advance and take advantage of all available resources to meet deadlines and even submit proposals early. In other words, they have developed a controlled approach to federal grantseeking.

The federal government grants over $85 billion each year. Its system follows a yearly cycle that I refer to as the Federal Grants Clock (Figure 7.1).

Referring to the clock, application packages are usually sent (position A) to prospective grantees four to eight weeks before the completed applications are due (B), and after the proposals are reviewed (C), grants are usually awarded six months to one year after submission (D). The key to proactive government grantseeking is knowing *what else* occurs on the clock (E) and how your actions can dramatically increase your success rate while decreasing the madness associated with a last-minute rush to meet a deadline.

Do not wait to learn about a grant opportunity; do not postpone preparing your proposal until you receive an application package. *Start*

Figure 7.1

THE $85 BILLION FEDERAL GRANTS CLOCK™

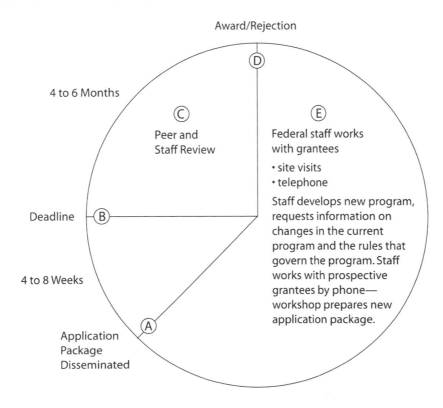

The clock operates Monday through Friday (except federal holidays) 52 weeks per year. The federal government's year begins on October 1 and ends September 30.

early! To do so, you need to have a working knowledge of the basic grant-information publications.

The Catalog of Federal Domestic Assistance

In the fall of each year the federal government publishes the *Catalog of Federal Domestic Assistance* (CFDA). It lists more than 1,300 granting programs that disseminate approximately $80 billion in grants annually and provides the grantseeker with all sorts of valuable information, including deadlines.

The CFDA is available on the Internet; access is available on-line to all 1,300 plus programs. The Department of Education has a search tool on its website that includes the CFDA. Go to www.ed.gov and click on the Programs and Services icon. There you will find a link to the CFDA that is updated fairly often. You may also purchase the CFDA from the Superintendent of Documents, U.S. Government Printing Office (202-512-1800), for under $100. However, you do not have to buy your own copy. The CFDA is provided free to at least two libraries in each congressional district. (Your congressperson should know which libraries have been designated Federal Depository Libraries.) Most public libraries also have copies, as do college and university libraries and grants offices.

Why should you use the CFDA? Even if you are planning to pursue only foundation or corporate grants, you should be knowledgeable about existing federal programs for your project area. So armed, you are able to explain to a prospective private grantor why you are approaching it instead of a federal agency. For instance, if you know for certain that there are no federal program funds designated for your project area or that federal funding is limited to three projects across the entire country, it will be easier for you to demonstrate why private grant support is so necessary.

The most efficient way to locate the granting agencies that represent your best opportunities is to use the key words you circled on your Key Words Worksheets and compare them with the indexes in the CFDA. The CFDA has five indexes, of which the Subject Index is the most helpful for locating grant opportunities in the Education Department and in other departments that have an interest in education.

In Chapter Five we discussed a project idea related to the use of parent-teacher-student involvement through electronic interface. In searching for federal grant opportunities for this project, we used educational technology, elementary education, and telecommunications as our key words and looked for program matches in the CFDA's indexes. By looking in the Functional and the Subject Indexes we matched our interests with this federal program:

CFDA 84.303   Technology Challenge Grants

Exhibit 7.3 shows CFDA 84.303 to help you understand the federal grants system. This understanding is crucial to the development of a proactive grantseeking system that will enable you to start the process early and make preproposal contact with the appropriate funding agency.

In the example—CFDA 84.303 Technology Challenge Grants— reader aids have been numbered in the left margin to coincide with the numbers that follow.

1. Program Title: Technology Challenge Grants

2. Federal Agency: This tells you the arm of the government that handles this program. Many of your grant programs will be sponsored by the Department of Education, but you may also apply to the National Science Foundation, the National Endowment for the Arts, and so on.

3. Authorization: This tells you the source of the funding.

4. Objectives: This section is important because it gives you the first indication of the appropriateness of your idea in relationship to the funding program. In the example of a project to increase parent, teacher, and student involvement through electronic interface, application to this program would be appropriate if the project promoted the use of technology to support school reform, improve student learning, and develop professionals in the integration of technology into school curriculum.

5. Types of Assistance: This program funds project grants. You must know what types of assistance are provided to determine if the federal program is interested in funding projects or research or if it funds by a formula that allocates money to eligible recipients through predetermined criteria.

6. User and Use Restrictions: User and use restrictions help you further determine if the program is an appropriate source of funds for your project.

7. Eligibility Requirements:

- *Applicant Eligibility*—This section tells you that your school is an eligible recipient if it has been designated as an LEA. If your school is not eligible, this section tells you whom you should develop a relationship with to submit your proposal through that organization.

- *Beneficiary Eligibility*—This section tells you what type of individual or organization is intended to benefit from the project.

- *Credentials/Documentation*—The Office of Management and Budget (OMB) publishes several management booklets that outline the rules for requesting, spending, and documenting expenditures under a federal grant.

Exhibit 7.3

① **84.303 TECHNOLOGY CHALLENGE GRANTS**

② **FEDERAL AGENCY: ASSISTANT SECRETARY FOR EDUCATION RESEARCH, STATISTICS, AND IMPROVEMENT, DEPARTMENT OF EDUCATION**

③ **AUTHORIZATION:** Elementary and Secondary Education Act of 1965, Title III, Part A, Section 3136, as amended, 20 U.S.C. 6846.

④ **OBJECTIVES:** The grants under this program support the development, interconnection, implementation, improvement, and maintenance of an effective educational technology infrastructure, including activities to provide equipment, training for teachers, school library and media personnel, and technical support. The primary goals of the program are to promote the use of technology to support school reform, support network and telecommunication connections to improve student learning, and support professional development in the integration of high-quality technology into the school curriculum.

⑤ **TYPES OF ASSISTANCE:** Project Grants (Discretionary).

⑥ **USES AND USE RESTRICTIONS:** Priority is given to applications that (1) serve areas with a high percentage of disadvantaged students or with the greatest need for educational technology and directly benefit students; (2) ensure ongoing, sustained, professional development to further the use of technology in schools; (3) ensure effective and sustainable use of the technologies acquired; and (4) contribute substantial financial and other resources to achieve the goals of the project.

⑦ **ELIGIBILITY REQUIREMENTS:**
Applicant Eligibility: Consortia may apply. Consortia must include at least one local educational agency (LEA) with a high percentage or number of children living below the poverty line and may include other LEAs, state educational agencies, institutions of higher education, businesses, academic content experts, software designers, museums, libraries, or other entities.
Beneficiary Eligibility: Elementary and secondary education students and teachers benefit.
Credentials/Documentation: None.

⑧ **APPLICATION AND AWARD PROCESS:**
Preapplication Coordination: This program is eligible for coverage under E.O. 12372, "Intergovernmental Review of Federal Programs." An applicant should consult the office or official designated as the single point of contact in his or her state for more information on the process the state requires to be followed in applying for assistance, if the state has selected the program for review.
Application Procedure: Application forms and instructions are available from the program office. Application deadlines and other information for applicants are published in the *Federal Register*. Contact the program office for information.
Award Procedure: Awards are competitively selected following review by nonfederal experts and by program staff. The Assistant Secretary for the Office of Educational Research and Improvement approves the selection. Information on the award process is available from the program office.
Deadlines: Applicant deadlines and other information for applicants are published as a notice in the *Federal Register*. The deadline notice is included in the application package.
Range of Approval/Disapproval Time: The estimated time is 120 days.
Appeals: Not applicable.
Renewals: As required by the Education Department General Administrative Regulations (EDGAR) for direct grant programs (see 34 CFR 75.253). Generally, for multiple-year awards, continuation awards after the first budget period are made if: sufficient funds have been appropriated; the recipient has either made substantial progress in meeting the goals of the project or obtained approval for changes in the project; the recipient has submitted all required reports; and continuation is in the best interest of the government.

(continued)

Exhibit 7.3 (continued)

(9) **ASSISTANCE CONSIDERATIONS:**

Formula and Matching Requirements: None.

Length and Time Phasing of Assistance: After an initial 12-month competitively selected award, four additional years may be awarded. The maximum length of time an award may last is five years. Awards are subject to the availability of funds.

(10) **POST ASSISTANCE REQUIREMENTS:**

Reports: As required by the Education Department General Administrative Regulations (EDGAR) for direct programs (34 CFR 75). Generally, annual performance and financial reports are required. Reporting will be included in the grant award document.

Audits: See 34 CFR 74.26. Institutions of higher education and nonprofit organizations are subject to the audit requirements of OMB Circular No. A-133. State and local governments are subject to the requirements in the Single Audit Act and the Department of Education regulations implementing OMB Circular No. A-128.

Records: As required by EDGAR, for direct grant programs (34 CFR 75). Generally, records related to grant funds, compliance, and performance must be maintained for a period of five years after completion. As required by EDGAR, to maintain appropriate records and related grant funds.

(11) **FINANCIAL INFORMATION:**

Account Identification: 18-1100-0-1-503.

Obligations: (Grants) FY 96 $38,000,000; FY 97 est $56,965,000; and FY 98 est $75,000,000.

Range and Average of Financial Assistance: $500,000 to $2,000,000 per year (average $1,000,000 per year) for five years.

(12) **PROGRAM ACCOMPLISHMENTS:** Almost 600 applications were received and 24 grants were made in fiscal year 1996. 19 additional grants were continued. Approximately 300 districts participated in the program in fiscal year 1996.

(13) **REGULATIONS, GUIDELINES, AND LITERATURE:** Education Department General Administrative Regulations (EDGAR), 34 CFR 74, 75, 77, 78, 79, 80, 81, 82, 85, and 86. Information on regulations are included in the application package and are available from the program office.

(14) **INFORMATION CONTACTS:**

Regional or Local Office: Not applicable.

Headquarters Office: Challenge Grants for Technology in Education, Office of Educational Research and Improvement, 555 New Jersey Avenue, NW, Washington, DC 2028-5544. Contact: Thomas Carroll, Director, Challenge Grants Program, Telephone: (202) 208-3882.

(15) **RELATED PROGRAMS:** None.

(16) **EXAMPLES OF FUNDED PROJECTS:** A project in Towanda, PA uses interactive video-conferencing to provide services to 23 small rural school districts serving 45,000 students in PA, NY, and NJ. A project in Waukegan is promoting improved learning in math and science for 7,000 students in grades 4 through 12 by the use of multimedia computers in classrooms and Internet connections. In addition, the project is establishing technology learning community centers for students and adults to access job opportunities.

(17) **CRITERIA FOR SELECTING PROPOSALS:** Applications are reviewed on the basis of their significance and feasibility. Detailed selection criteria are included in the application package.

8. Application and Award Process:

- *Preapplication Coordination*—This section outlines the OMB requirements related to your state's review and knowledge of your proposal. If you have a district grants office, it will know whom to contact in your state office concerning this matter.

- *Application Procedure*—This describes the rules for submittal.

- *Award Procedure*—This section tells you who will review and approve your proposal. Proposals submitted to this particular program will be read by program staff and nonfederal experts.

- *Deadlines*—Established by notice published in the *Federal Register.* The *Register* is explained immediately following this CFDA example.

- *Range of Approval/Disapproval Time*—Closing date published in the *Federal Register.*

- *Appeals*—In this case, there is no procedure for appealing the grant's decision. Some federal programs have a specific appeal procedure.

- *Renewals*—This information is important when you are planning a project that may take several years. In this case, a grant recipient is eligible for continuation of its award after the first budget period if it meets certain criteria.

9. Assistance Considerations:

- *Formula and Matching Requirements*—This section outlines what portion of the project costs will be borne by your school district. It is vital that you have a plan for the match and your school's endorsement that it will commit this share. In this example, there are no matching requirements.

- *Length and Time Phasing of Assistance*—In this case, after the initial twelve months, four additional years may be awarded.

10. Post-Assistance Requirements: Your district will be required to make reports and maintain records and may be subject to audits. Don't let this section scare you. Your business office will handle it.

11. Financial Information:
- *Account Identification*—Account identification number.

- *Obligations*—By reviewing this section, you can determine if the program is slated to increase or decrease its funding level. Note that the estimated 1998 budget for this program was $75 million, but amounts can be changed drastically by Congress. In this example, program funds went up.

- *Range and Average of Financial Assistance*—In 1996 the range was $500,000 to $2 million for five years, with the average award being $1 million per year. This should indicate to you that this program is not your best choice if you are requesting $25,000 per year.

12. Program Accomplishments: This section gives you important information on previously selected grantees and on the number of awards made in the past. In this case, twenty-four new awards were made in 1996 and nineteen more were continued. This section also informs you if the program is being phased out. For example, it may say "no new awards."

13. Regulations, Guidelines, and Literature: This section tells you where the rules and guides can be found and what administrative regulation they follow. Most of the rules pertain to your district personnel and business office and compliance should be discussed with your district grants office or administration.

14. Information Contacts:

- *Regional or Local Office*—Most regional offices were closed during the federal cutbacks of the early 1980s.

- *Headquarters Office*—This section provides the contact name, address, and phone number you will need if you select this funder as a possible source of funds for your project.

15. Related Programs: This section lists the CFDA names and digit codes of other sources of funds that have similar target populations or objectives. In this case none are listed.

16. Examples of Funded Projects: This section provides a sample of the solutions that the grantor valued highly enough to fund.

17. Criteria for Selecting Proposals: This section tells you where the criteria that the agency will follow in the evaluation procedure can be found. In this case, selection criteria are included in the application package. Each agency has its own criteria, and criteria may differ between programs.

The Federal Register

The *Federal Register* is the federal government's daily newspaper. For a teacher, this resource could cause a severe case of cognitive overload. You should not read this publication daily. You just need to know its purpose as it relates to federal grantseeking.

The *Register* provides the government with a way to solicit feedback on the rules that governed the previous year's grant solicitation and award process. It is not unusual for the federal agency to publish the previous year's rules six months before the next deadline to solicit the public's opinions on the way the proposals are awarded.

A period of thirty days is usually given to comment on the rules. The agency reviews the comments and may make changes based on them. The public is then allowed another thirty days to comment on the changes before the final rules are printed. These rules govern the program's priorities and the scoring or review system; they also provide valuable insight into exactly what the agency is looking for.

Being aware of this process gives you a strong advantage over your competitors. You now know that there is no need to wait around until you receive a formal application package. You know that you can telephone a federal program officer to ask when information on the rules and the deadline was printed in the *Federal Register*. The information you obtain from the CFDA and *Register* enables you to make a decision on the appropriateness of the funding opportunity, and you can get started!

You can use your new knowledge concerning the two most basic federal grants publications, the CFDA and *Federal Register*, to look like a grants pro. For example, assume that you have used your key words and the CFDA indexes to determine that CFDA 84-303, Technology Challenge Grants, looks like a good potential funding source for your project. You could contact Thomas Carroll, the information contact listed in the CFDA, to ask if the deadline has been announced yet and if it hasn't, when he thinks it will appear in the *Federal Register*. You could also ask him if any notices have been published in the *Register* that could assist you, such as comments on the rules and so on.

If, for example, you contacted Carroll in December, he may have informed you that the notice to invite applications was to be printed in January and that the application deadline was expected to be March. Clearly, you would be a step ahead of your competitors and gain significant insight by obtaining a copy of the January *Federal Register*.

You must know the exact day that the rules were printed. In this case, it was March 5, 1998. Frequently the federal agency will reproduce this *Federal Register* and include it in the application package. You can gain access to the *Register* on the internet at http://gcs.ed.gov/fedreg.htm.

Foundation Research Tools

The Foundation Center Library National Collections and field offices offer the best available selection of information on foundation and corporate grants. The National Collections are located in New York City and Washington, D.C. The field offices are located in Cleveland, San Francisco, and Atlanta. To help nonprofit organizations that are not able to gain access to the National Collections and field offices, cooperating collections have been established in libraries, community foundations, and even some nonprofit agencies throughout the United States. The organizations that house the cooperating collections do not get paid to do so, although they do receive the publications for free. Use Exhibit 7.4 to locate the collection nearest you and take advantage of its many reference books on foundation funding.

The most useful book will be a foundation book that focuses on your state. Most states have a state directory, which you can find at your cooperating collection.

The Foundation Center publishes several popular grants reference materials, including the *Foundation Directory*. Available at your Foundation Center Regional Library, this yearly publication is the most important single reference work on grantmaking foundations in the United States. The 1998 edition is the twentieth. To be included in the *Directory*, a foundation must either have assets of at least $2 million or make grants in excess of $200,000 annually. Over 8,600 of the existing 45,000 foundations have met at least one of these criteria and are included in the *Directory*.

The Foundation Directory, Part 2 is also a very important publication. It describes over 4,900 foundations that make annual grants of up to $200,000 but over $50,000.

Both the *Foundation Directory* and *Foundation Directory, Part 2* are indexed five ways:

- *Foundation Name*—If you know the name of a foundation that may be interested in elementary or middle school education, you can locate it in the directories using this index. The index entry itself provides one crucial piece of information: the state in which the foundation is registered. You need to know this to locate the foundation in the directories, as the entries are in alphabetical order by state.

- *Subject Area*—Your Key Words Worksheet will provide you with the words you need to use this index and locate the foundations interested in your particular area. Elementary education is becoming increasingly popular as a subject of funding.

- *Types of Support*—Many foundations have severe restrictions on the types of funding they will support. This index enables you to quickly discover this important information.

- *Donors, Trustees, and Officers*—This index provides information that may help you develop linkages with foundations.

- *Geographic*—Foundations are listed under the state in which they are located. Foundations in boldface type make grants on a national, regional, or international basis. The others generally limit giving to the city or state in which they are located.

Exhibit 7.4

FOUNDATION CENTER COOPERATING COLLECTIONS

The Foundation Center is an independent national service organization established by foundations to provide an authoritative source of information on foundation and corporate giving. The New York, Washington, D.C., Atlanta, Cleveland, and San Francisco reference collections operated by the Foundation Center offer a wide variety of services and comprehensive collections of information on foundations and grants. Cooperating Collections are libraries, community foundations, and other nonprofit agencies that provide a core collection of Foundation Center publications and a variety of supplementary materials and services in areas useful to grantseekers. The core collection consists of:

THE FOUNDATION DIRECTORY 1 AND 2, AND
   SUPPLEMENT
THE FOUNDATION 1000
FOUNDATION FUNDAMENTALS
FOUNDATION GIVING
THE FOUNDATION GRANTS INDEX

THE FOUNDATION GRANTS INDEX
   QUARTERLY
FOUNDATION GRANTS TO INDIVIDUALS
GUIDE TO U.S. FOUNDATIONS, THEIR TRUSTEES,
   OFFICERS, AND DONORS
THE FOUNDATION CENTER'S GUIDE TO
   PROPOSAL WRITING

NATIONAL DIRECTORY OF CORPORATE
   GIVING
NATIONAL DIRECTORY OF GRANTMAKING
   PUBLIC CHARITIES
NATIONAL GUIDE TO FUNDING IN ... (SERIES)
USER-FRIENDLY GUIDE

All five Center libraries have FC Search The Foundation Center's Database on CD-ROM available for patron use, and most Cooperating Collections have it as well, as noted by the symbol (+). Also, many of the network members make available for public use sets of private foundation information returns (IRS Form 99-PF) for their state and/or neighboring states noted by the symbol (*). A complete set of U.S. foundation returns can be found at the New York and Washington D.C., offices of the Foundation Center. The Atlanta, Cleveland, and San Francisco offices contain IRS Form 990-PF returns for the southeastern, midwestern, and western states respectively. Because the collections vary in their hours, materials, and services, it's recommended that you call the collection in advance. To check on new locations or current holdings, call toll-free 1-800-424-9836, or visit our Web site at http://fdncenter.org/library/library.html.

Participants in the Foundation Center's Cooperating Collections network are libraries or nonprofit information centers that provide fundraising information and other funding-related technical assistance in their communities. Cooperating Collections agree to provide free public access to a basic collection of Foundation Center publications during a regular schedule of hours, offering free funding research guidance to all visitors. Many also provide a variety of services for local nonprofit organizations, using staff or volunteers to prepare special materials, organize workshops, or conduct orientations.

The Foundation Center welcomes inquiries from libraries or information centers in the U.S. interested in providing this type of public information service. If you are interested in establishing a funding information library for the use of nonprofit organizations in your area or in learning more about the program, please write to: Rich Romeo, Coordinator of Cooperating Collections, The Foundation Center, 79 Fifth Avenue, New York, NY 10003-3076.

REFERENCE COLLECTIONS OPERATED BY THE FOUNDATION CENTER

THE FOUNDATION CENTER
8th Floor
79 Fifth Ave.
New York, NY 10003
(212) 620-4230

THE FOUNDATION CENTER
312 Sutter St., Rm. 312
San Francisco, CA 94108
(415) 397-0902

THE FOUNDATION CENTER
1001 Connecticut Ave., NW
Washington, DC 20036
(202) 331-1400

THE FOUNDATION CENTER
Kent H. Smith Library
1422 Euclid, Suite 1356
Cleveland, OH 44115
(216) 861-1933

THE FOUNDATION CENTER
Suite 150, Grand Lobby
Hurt Bldg., 50 Hurt Plaza
Atlanta, GA 30303
(404) 880-0094

ALABAMA

BIRMINGHAM PUBLIC LIBRARY*+
Government Documents
2100 Park Place
Birmingham 35203
(205) 226-3600

HUNTSVILLE PUBLIC LIBRARY+
915 Monroe St.
Huntsville 35801
(205) 532-5940

UNIVERSITY OF SOUTH ALABAMA*
Library Building
Mobile 36688
(205) 460-7025

AUBURN UNIVERSITY AT
MONTGOMERY LIBRARY*+
7300 University Dr.
Montgomery 36117-3596
(205) 244-3653

ALASKA

UNIVERSITY OF ALASKA AT
ANCHORAGE*+
Library
3211 Providence Dr.
Anchorage 99508
(907) 786-1848

JUNEAU PUBLIC LIBRARY+
Reference
292 Marine Way
Juneau 99801
(907) 586-5267

ARIZONA

PHOENIX PUBLIC LIBRARY*+
Information Services Department
1221 N. Central
Phoenix 85004
(602) 262-4636

TUCSON PIMA LIBRARY*+
101 N. Stone Ave.
Tucson 87501
(520) 791-4010

ARKANSAS

WESTARK COMMUNITY COLLEGE-
BORHAM LIBRARY*+
5210 Grand Ave.
Ft. Smith 72913
(501) 788-7200

CENTRAL ARKANSAS
LIBRARY SYSTEM*+
700 Louisiana
Little Rock 72201
(501) 370-5952

PINE BLUFF-JEFFERSON COUNTY
LIBRARY SYSTEM
200 E Eighth
Pine Bluff 71601
(501) 534-2159

CALIFORNIA

HUMBOLDT AREA FOUNDATION*+
P.O. Box 99
Bayside 95524
(707) 442-2993

VENTURA COUNTY COMMUNITY
FOUNDATION*+
Funding and Information Resource
Center
1355 Del Norte Rd.,
Suite 150
Camarillo 93030
(805) 988-0196

FRESNO REGIONAL FOUNDATION+
Nonprofit Advancement Ctr
1999 Tuolumne St., Suite 650
Fresno 93721
(209) 498-3929

CALIFORNIA COMMUNITY
FOUNDATION*+
Funding Information Center
606 S. Olive St., Suite 2400
Los Angeles 90014-1526
(213) 413-4042

EAST BAY RESOURCE CENTER FOR
NONPROFIT SUPPORT+
1203 Preservation Pkwy., Suite 100
Oakland 94612
(510) 834-1010

GRANT & RESOURCE CENTER OF
NORTHERN CALIFORNIA*+
Building C, Suite A
2280 Benton Dr.
Redding 96003
(916) 244-1219

LOS ANGELES PUBLIC LIBRARY
West Valley Regional Banch Library
19036 Van Owen St.
Reseda 91335
(818) 345-4393

RIVERSIDE PUBLIC LIBRARY
3581 Mission Inn Ave.
Riverside 92501
(909) 782-5202

Exhibit 7.4 (continued)

NONPROFIT RESOURCE CENTER+
Sacramento Public Library
828 I St., 2nd Floor
Sacramento 95814
(916) 264-2772

SAN DIEGO FOUNDATION*+
Funding Information Center
1420 Kettner Blvd., Suite 500
San Diego 92101
(619) 239-8815

NONPROFIT DEVELOPMENT
CENTER+
1922 The Alameda, Suite 212
San Jose 95126
(408) 248-9505

PENINSULA COMMUNITY
FOUNDATION*+
Peninsula Nonprofit Center
1700 S. El Camino Real, R201
San Mateo 94402-3049
(650) 358-9392

LOS ANGELES PUBLIC LIBRARY+
San Pedro Regional Branch
9131 S. Gaffey St.
San Pedro 90731
(310) 548-7779

VOLUNTEER CENTER OF GREATER
ORANGE COUNTY+
Nonprofit Management Assistance
Center
1901 E. 4th St., Ste. 100
Santa Ana 92705
(714) 953-1655

SANTA BARBARA PUBLIC LIBRARY+
40 E. Anapamu St.
Santa Barbara 93101
(805) 962-7653

SANTA MONICA PUBLIC LIBRARY+
1343 Sixth St.
Santa Monica 90401-1603
(310) 458-8600

SONOMA COUNTY LIBRARY+
3rd & E Sts.
Santa Rosa 95404
(707) 545-0831

SEASIDE BRANCH LIBRARY+
550 Harcourt St.
Seaside 93955
(408) 899-8131

COLORADO

EL POMAR NONPROFIT RESOURCE
CENTER+
1661 Mesa Ave.
Colorado Springs 80906
(800) 554-7711

DENVER PUBLIC LIBRARY*+
General Reference
10 West 14th Ave. Pkwy.
Denver 80204
(303) 640-6200

CONNECTICUT

DANBURY PUBLIC LIBRARY+
170 Main St.
Danbury 06810
(203) 797-4527

GREENWICH LIBRARY*+
101 Putnam Ave.
Greenwich 06830
(203) 622-7910

HARTFORD PUBLIC LIBRARY*+
500 Main St.
Hartford 06103
(860) 543-8656

NEW HAVEN FREE PUBLIC
LIBRARY+
Reference Dept.
133 Elm St.
New Haven 06510-2057
(203) 946-8130

DELAWARE

UNIVERSITY OF DELAWARE *+
Hugh Morris Library
Newark 19717-5267
(302) 831-2432

FLORIDA

VOLUSIA COUNTY LIBRARY
CENTER+
City Island
Daytona Beach 32014-4484
(904) 257-6036

NOVA SOUTHEASTERN
UNIVERSITY*+
Einstein Library
3301 College Ave.
Fort Lauderdale 33314
(954) 262-4601

INDIAN RIVER COMMUNITY
COLLEGE+
Charles S. Miley Learning Resource
Center
3209 Virginia Ave.
Fort Pierce 34981-5599
(561) 462-4757

JACKSONVILLE PUBLIC
LIBRARIES*+
Grants Resource Center
122 N. Ocean St.
Jacksonville 32202
(904) 630-2665

MIAMI-DADE PUBLIC LIBRARY*+
Humanities/Social Science
101 W. Flagler St.
Miami 33130
(305) 375-5575

ORLANDO PUBLIC LIBRARY*
Social Sciences Department
101 E. Central Blvd.
Orlando 32801
(407) 425-4694

SELBY PUBLIC LIBRARY
Reference
1001 Blvd. of the Arts
Sarasota 34236
(941) 316-1183

TAMPA-HILLSBOROUGH COUNTY
PUBLIC LIBRARY*+
900 N. Ashley Drive
Tampa 33602
(813) 273-3628

COMMUNITY FDN. OF PALM
BEACH & MARTIN COUNTIES*
324 Datura St., Suite 340
West Palm Beach 33401
(407) 659-6800

GEORGIA

ATLANTA-FULTON PUBLIC
LIBRARY*+
Foundation Collection—
Ivan Allen Department
1 Margaret Mitchell Square
Atlanta 30303-1089
(404) 730-1900

UNITED WAY OF CENTRAL
GEORGIA*+
Community Resource Center
301 Mulberry Street, Suite 301
Macon 31201
(912) 745-4732

SAVANNAH STATE UNIVERSITY
LIBRARY+
Savannah 31404
(912) 356-2693

THOMAS COUNTY PUBLIC
LIBRARY*+
201 N. Madison St.
Thomasville 31792
(912) 225-5252

HAWAII

UNIVERSITY OF HAWAII*+
Hamilton Library
2550 The Mall
Honolulu 96822
(808) 956-7214

HAWAII COMMUNITY
FOUNDATION RESOURCE
LIBRARY+
900 Fort St., Suite 1300
Honolulu 96813
(808) 537-6333

IDAHO

BOISE PUBLIC LIBRARY*+
715 S. Capitol Blvd.
Boise 83702
(208) 384-4024

CALDWELL PUBLIC LIBRARY*+
1010 Dearborn St.
Caldwell 83605
(208) 459-3242

ILLINOIS

DONORS FORUM OF CHICAGO*+
New Address:
208 South LaSalle, Suite 740
Chicago 60604
(312) 431-0265

EVANSTON PUBLIC LIBRARY*+
1703 Orrington Ave.
Evanston 60201
(847) 866-0305

ROCK ISLAND PUBLIC LIBRARY+
401 - 19th St.
Rock Island 61201
(309) 788-7627

UNIVERSITY OF ILLINOIS AT
SPRINGFIELD*+
Brookens Library
Shepherd Road
Springfield 62794-9243
(217) 786-6633

INDIANA

EVANSVILLE-VANDERBURGH
COUNTY PUBLIC LIBRARY+
22 Southeast Fifth St.
Evansville 47708
(812) 428-8200

ALLEN COUNTY PUBLIC LIBRARY*+
900 Webster St.
Ft. Wayne 46802
(219) 424-0544

INDIANA UNIVERSITY NORTHWEST
LIBRARY+
3400 Broadway
Gary 46408
(219) 980-6582

INDIANAPOLIS-MARION COUNTY
PUBLIC LIBRARY*+
Social Sciences
40 E. St. Clair
Indianapolis 46206
(317) 269-1733

VIGO COUNTY PUBLIC LIBRARY+
1 Library Square
Terre Haute 47807
(812) 232-1113

IOWA

CEDAR RAPIDS PUBLIC LIBRARY*
Foundation Center Collection
500 First St., SE
Cedar Rapids 52401
(319) 398-5123

SOUTHWESTERN COMMUNITY
COLLEGE*+
Learning Resource Center
1501 W. Townline Rd.
Creston 50801
(515) 782-7081

PUBLIC LIBRARY OF DES
MOINES*+
100 Locust St.
Des Moines 50309-1791
(515) 283-4152

(continued)

Exhibit 7.4 (continued)

SIOUX CITY PUBLIC LIBRARY*+
529 Pierce St.
Sioux City 51101-1202
(712) 252-5669

KANSAS

DODGE CITY PUBLIC LIBRARY*+
1001 2nd Ave.
Dodge City 67801
(316) 225-0248

TOPEKA AND SHAWNEE COUNTY
PUBLIC LIBRARY*+
1515 SW 10th Ave.
Topeka 66604-1374
(913) 233-2040

WICHITA PUBLIC LIBRARY*+
223 S. Main St.
Wichita 67202
(316) 262-0611

KENTUCKY

WESTERN KENTUCKY UNIVERSITY+
Helm-Cravens Library
Bowling Green 42101-3576
(502) 745-6125

LEXINGTON PUBLIC LIBRARY*
140 East Main Street
Lexington 40507-1376
(606) 231-5520

LOUISVILLE FREE PUBLIC
LIBRARY*+
301 York Street
Louisville 40203
(502) 574-1611

LOUISIANA

EAST BATON ROUGE PARISH
LIBRARY*+
Centroplex Branch Grants
Collection
120 St. Louis
Baton Rouge 70802
(504) 389-4960

BEAUREGARD PARISH LIBRARY*+
205 S. Washington Ave.
De Ridder 70634
(318) 463-6217

NEW ORLEANS PUBLIC LIBRARY*+
Business & Science Division
219 Loyola Ave.
New Orleans 70140
(504) 596-2580

SHREVE MEMORIAL LIBRARY*
424 Texas St.
Shreveport 71120-1523
(318) 226-5894

MAINE

MAINE GRANTS INFORMATION
CENTER*+
University of Southern Maine
Library
314 Forrest Ave.
Portland 04104-9301
(207) 780-5029

MARYLAND

ENOCH PRATT FREE LIBRARY*+
Social Science & History
400 Cathedral St.
Baltimore 21201
(410) 396-5430

MASSACHUSETTS

ASSOCIATED GRANTMAKERS OF
MASSACHUSETTS*+
294 Washington St., Suite 840
Boston 02108
(617) 426-2606

BOSTON PUBLIC LIBRARY*+
Soc. Sci. Reference
700 Boylston St., R1069
Boston 02117
(617) 536-5400

WESTERN MASSACHUSETTS
FUNDING RESOURCE CENTER+
65 Elliot St.
Springfield 01101-1730
(413) 732-3175

WORCESTER PUBLIC LIBRARY*+
Grants Resource Center
Salem Square
Worcester 01608
(508) 799-1655

MICHIGAN

ALPENA COUNTY LIBRARY*+
211 N. First St.
Alpena 49707
(517) 356-6188

UNIVERSITY OF MICHIGAN-ANN
ARBOR*+
Graduate Library
Reference & Research Services
Department
Ann Arbor 48109-1205
(313) 764-9373

WILLARD PUBLIC LIBRARY*+
7 West Van Buren St.
Battle Creek 49017
(616) 968-8166

HENRY FORD CENTENNIAL
LIBRARY*+
Adult Services
16301 Michigan Ave.
Dearborn 48126
(313) 943-2330

WAYNE STATE UNIVERSITY*+
Purdy/Kresge Library
5265 Cass Avenue
Detroit 48202
(313) 577-6424

MICHIGAN STATE UNIVERSITY
LIBRARIES*+
Social Sciences/Humanities
Main Library
East Lansing 48824-1048
(517) 353-8818

FARMINGTON COMMUNITY
LIBRARY*+
32737 West 12 Mile Rd.
Farmington Hills 48018
(810) 553-0300

UNIVERSITY OF MICHIGAN-FLINT*
Library
Flint 48502-2186
(810) 762-3408

GRAND RAPIDS PUBLIC LIBRARY*+
Business Dept., 3rd Floor
60 Library Plaza NE
Grand Rapids 49503-3093
(616) 456-3600

MICHIGAN TECHNOLOGICAL
UNIVERSITY+
Van Pelt Library
1400 Townsend Dr.
Houghton 49931
(906) 487-2507

MAUD PRESTON PALENSKE
MEMORIAL LIBRARY+
500 Market St.
St. Joseph 49085
(616) 983-7167

NORTHWESTERN MICHIGAN
COLLEGE*+
Mark & Helen Osterin Library
1701 E. Front St.
Traverse City 49684
(616) 922-1060

MINNESOTA

DULUTH PUBLIC LIBRARY*+
520 W. Superior St.
Duluth 55802
(218) 723-3802

SOUTHWEST STATE UNIVERSITY*+
University Library
Marshall 56258
(507) 537-6176

MINNEAPOLIS PUBLIC LIBRARY*+
Sociology Department
300 Nicollet Mall
Minneapolis 55401
(612) 630-6300

ROCHESTER PUBLIC LIBRARY
11 First St. SE
Rochester 55904-3777
(507) 285-8002

ST. PAUL PUBLIC LIBRARY+
90 W. Fourth St.
St. Paul 55102
(612) 266-7000

MISSISSIPPI

JACKSON/HINDS LIBRARY
SYSTEM*+
300 N. State St.
Jackson 39201
(601) 968-5803

MISSOURI

CLEARINGHOUSE FOR MIDCONTI-
NENT FOUNDATIONS*+
University of Missouri - Kansas City
5110 Cherry, Suite 310
Kansas City 64110
(816) 235-1176

KANSAS CITY PUBLIC LIBRARY*+
311 E. 12th St.
Kansas City 64106-2454
(816) 221-9650

METROPOLITAN ASSOCIATION FOR
PHILANTHROPY, INC.*+
1 Metropolitan Square, Suite 1295
St. Louis 63102
(314) 621-6220

SPRINGFIELD-GREENE COUNTY
LIBRARY*+
397 E. Central
Springfield 65802
(417) 837-5000

MONTANA

MONTANA STATE UNIVERSITY -
BILLINGS*+
Library-Special Collections
1500 North 30th St.
Billings 59101-0298
(406) 657-2046

BOZEMAN PUBLIC LIBRARY*+
220 E. Lamme
Bozeman 59715
(406) 586-4787

MONTANA STATE LIBRARY*+
Library Services
1515 E. 6th Ave.
Helena 59620
(406) 444-3004

UNIVERSITY OF MONTANA*+
Maureen & Mike Mansfield Library
Missoula 59812-1195
(406) 243-6800

NEBRASKA

UNIVERSITY OF NEBRASKA-
LINCOLN*+
Love Library
14th & R Sts.
Lincoln 68588-0410
(402) 472-2848

W. DALE CLARK LIBRARY*+
Social Sciences Department
215 S. 15th St.
Omaha 68102
(402) 444-4826

NEVADA

LAS VEGAS-CLARK COUNTY
LIBRARY DISTRICT*+
1401 E. Flamingo
Las Vegas 89119
(702) 733-3642

WASHOE COUNTY LIBRARY*+
301 S. Center St.
Reno 89501
(702) 785-4010

NEW HAMPSHIRE

PLYMOUTH STATE COLLEGE*+
Herbert H. Lamson Library
Plymouth 03264
(603) 535-2258

CONCORD COUNTY LIBRARY
45 Green St.
Concord 03301
(603) 225-8670

Exhibit 7.4 (continued)

NEW JERSEY

CUMBERLAND COUNTY LIBRARY+
New Jersey Room
800 E. Commerce St.
Bridgeton 08302
(609) 453-2210

FREE PUBLIC LIBRARY OF
ELIZABETH*+
11 S. Broad St.
Elizabeth 07202
(908) 354-6060

COUNTY COLLEGE OF MORRIS*+
Learning Resource Center
214 Center Grove Rd.
Randolph 07869
(201) 328-5296

NEW JERSEY STATE LIBRARY*+
Governmental Reference Services
185 West State St.
Trenton 08625-0520
(609) 292-6220

NEW MEXICO

ALBUQUERQUE COMMUNITY
FOUNDATION*
3301 Menual NE, Ste. 30
Albuquerque 87176-6960
(505) 883-6240

NEW MEXICO STATE LIBRARY*+
Information Services
1209 Camino Carlos Rey
Santa Fe 87505
(505) 476-9714

NEW YORK

NEW YORK STATE LIBRARY*+
Humanities Reference
Cultural Education Center
Empire State Plaza
Albany 12230
(518) 474-5355

SUFFOLK COOPERATIVE LIBRARY
SYSTEM+
627 N. Sunrise Service Rd.
Bellport 11713
(516) 286-1600

BRONX REFERENCE CENTER
New York Public Library
2556 Bainbridge Ave.
Bronx 10458
(718) 579-4257

THE NONPROFIT CONNECTION+
One Hanson Place, Room 1601
Brooklyn 11243
(718) 230-3200

BROOKLYN PUBLIC LIBRARY+
Social Sciences Division
Grand Army Plaza
Brooklyn 11238
(718) 780-7700

BUFFALO & ERIE COUNTY PUBLIC
LIBRARY*+
Business & Labor Dept.
Lafayette Square
Buffalo 14203
(716) 858-7097

HUNTINGTON PUBLIC LIBRARY+
338 Main St.
Huntington 11743
(516) 427-5165

QUEENS BOROUGH PUBLIC
LIBRARY+
Social Sciences Division
89-11 Merrick Blvd.
Jamaica 11432
(718) 990-0761

LEVITTOWN PUBLIC LIBRARY*+
1 Bluegrass Lane
Levittown 11756
(516) 731-5728

FOUNDATION CENTER OFFICE AND
LIBRARY+
79 Fifth Avenue, 8th Floor
New York 10003-3076
(212) 620-4230

NEW YORK PUBLIC LIBRARY+
Countee Cullen Branch Library
104 W. 136th St.
New York 10030
(212) 491-2070

ADRIANCE MEMORIAL LIBRARY+
Special Services Department
93 Market St.
Poughkeepsie 12601
(914) 485-3445

ROCHESTER PUBLIC LIBRARY*+
Social Sciences and Job
Information Center
115 South Avenue
Rochester 14604
(716) 428-8120

ONONDAGA COUNTY PUBLIC
LIBRARY+
447 S. Salina St.
Syracuse 13202-2494
(315) 435-1900

UTICA PUBLIC LIBRARY
303 Genesee St.
Utica 13501
(315) 735-2279

WHITE PLAINS PUBLIC LIBRARY+
100 Martine Ave.
White Plains 10601
(914) 422-1480

NORTH CAROLINA

COMMUNITY FDN. OF WESTERN
NORTH CAROLINA*+
Learning Resources Center
16 Biltmore Avenue, Suite 201
Asheville 28802
(704) 254-4960

THE DUKE ENDOWMENT*+
100 N. Tryon St., Suite 3500
Charlotte 28202
(704) 376-0291

DURHAM COUNTY PUBLIC
LIBRARY+
301 North Roxboro
Durham 27702
(919) 560-0110

STATE LIBRARY OF NORTH
CAROLINA*+
Government and Business Services
Archives Bldg., 109 E. Jones St.
Raleigh 27601
(919) 733-3270

FORSYTH COUNTY PUBLIC
LIBRARY*+
660 W. 5th St.
Winston-Salem 27101
(336) 727-2680

NORTH DAKOTA

BISMARCK PUBLIC LIBRARY
515 N. Fifth St.
Bismarck 58501
(701) 222-6410

FARGO PUBLIC LIBRARY*+
102 N. 3rd St.
Fargo 58102
(701) 241-1491

OHIO

STARK COUNTY DISTRICT
LIBRARY+
Humanities
715 Market Ave. N.
Canton 44702
(330) 452-0665

FOUNDATION CENTER OFFICE AND
LIBRARY
Kent H. Smith Library
Hanna Building, Suite 1356
1422 Euclid Avenue
Cleveland, OH 44115
(216) 861-1934

PUBLIC LIBRARY OF CINCINNATI &
HAMILTON COUNTY*+
Grants Resource Center
800 Vine St., Library Square
Cincinnati 45202-2071
(513) 369-6940

COLUMBUS METROPOLITAN
LIBRARY+
Business and Technology Dept.
96 S. Grant Ave.
Columbus 43215
(614) 645-2590

DAYTON & MONTGOMERY COUN-
TY PUBLIC LIBRARY*+
Grants Resource Center
215 E. Third St.
Dayton 45402
(937) 227-9500 x211

MANSFIELD/RICHLAND COUNTY
PUBLIC LIBRARY*+
42 West Third Street
Mansfield 44902
(419) 521-3110

TOLEDO-LUCAS COUNTY PUBLIC
LIBRARY*+
Social Sciences Department
325 Michigan St.
Toledo 43624-1614
(419) 259-5245

YOUNGSTOWN & MAHONING
COUNTY LIBRARY*+
305 Wick Ave.
Youngstown 44503

(330) 744-8636
MUSKINGUM COUNTY LIBRARY+
220 N. 5th St.
Zanesville 43701
(614) 453-0391

OKLAHOMA

OKLAHOMA CITY UNIVERSITY*+
Dulaney Browne Library
2501 N. Blackwelder
Oklahoma City 73106
(405) 521-5822

TULSA CITY-COUNTY LIBRARY*+
400 Civic Center
Tulsa 74103
(918) 596-7944

OREGON

OREGON INSTITUTE OF
TECHNOLOGY+
Library
3201 Campus Dr.
Klamath Falls 97601-8801
(503) 885-1773

PACIFIC NON-PROFIT NETWORK*+
Grantsmanship Resource Library
33 N. Central, Suite 211
Medford 97501
(541) 779-6044

MULTNOMAH COUNTY LIBRARY+
Government Documents
801 SW Tenth Ave.
Portland 97205
(503) 248-5123

OREGON STATE LIBRARY*+
State Library Building
Salem 97310
(503) 378-4277

PENNSYLVANIA

NORTHAMPTON COMMUNITY
COLLEGE+
Learning Resources Center
3835 Green Pond Rd.
Bethlehem 18017
(215) 861-5360

ERIE COUNTY LIBRARY+
Reference Department
160 East Front St.
Erie 16507-1554
(814) 451-6927

DAUPHIN COUNTY LIBRARY
SYSTEM+
Central Library
101 Walnut St.
Harrisburg 17101
(717) 234-4976

LANCASTER COUNTY PUBLIC
LIBRARY+
125 N. Duke St.
Lancaster 17602
(717) 394-2651

FREE LIBRARY OF PHILADELPHIA*+
Regional Foundation Center
Logan Square, 1901 Vine St.
Philadelphia 19103
(215) 686-5423

(continued)

Exhibit 7.4 (continued)

CARNEGIE LIBRARY OF
PITTSBURGH*+
Foundation Collection
4400 Forbes Ave.
Pittsburgh 15213-4080
(412) 622-1917

POCONO NORTHEAST DEVELOP-
MENT FUND+
James Pettinger Memorial Library
1151 Oak St.
Pittston 18640-3755
(717) 655-5581

READING PUBLIC LIBRARY+
100 South Fifth St.
Reading 19602
(610) 655-6355

MARTIN LIBRARY*+
159 Market St.
York 17401
(717) 846-5300

RHODE ISLAND

PROVIDENCE PUBLIC LIBRARY*+
225 Washington St.
Providence 02906
(401) 455-8088

SOUTH CAROLINA

ANDERSON COUNTY LIBRARY*+
202 East Greenville St.
Anderson 29621
(864) 260-4500

CHARLESTON COUNTY LIBRARY*+
404 King St.
Charleston 29403
(803) 723-1645

SOUTH CAROLINA STATE
LIBRARY*+
1500 Senate St.
Columbia 29211
(803) 734-8666

SOUTH DAKOTA

SOUTH DAKOTA STATE LIBRARY*+
800 Governors Dr.
Pierre 57501-2294
(605) 773-5070
(800) 592-1841 (SD residents)

NONPROFIT MANAGEMENT
INSTITUTE+
132 S. Dakota Rd.
Sioux Falls 57102
(605) 367-5380

SIOUXLAND LIBRARIES*+
201 N. Main Ave.
Sioux Falls 57102-1132
(605) 367-7081

TENNESSEE

KNOX COUNTY PUBLIC LIBRARY*+
500 W. Church Ave.
Knoxville 37902
(423) 544-5700

MEMPHIS & SHELBY COUNTY
PUBLIC LIBRARY*+
1850 Peabody Ave.
Memphis 38104
(901) 725-8877

NASHVILLE PUBLIC LIBRARY*+
Business Information Division
225 Polk Ave.
Nashville 37203
(615) 862-5843

TEXAS

NONPROFIT RESOURCE CENTER+
Funding Information Library
500 N. Chestnut, Suite 1511
Abilene 79604
(915) 677-8166

AMARILLO AREA FOUNDATION*+
700 First National Place
801 S. Fillmore
Amarillo 79101
(806) 376-4521

HOGG FOUNDATION FOR MENTAL
HEALTH*+
3001 Lake Austin Blvd.
Austin 78703
(512) 471-5041

FUNDING INFORMATION CENTER+
Beaumont Public Library
801 Pearl Street
Beaumont 77704
(409) 838-6606

CORPUS CHRISTI PUBLIC
LIBRARY*+
805 Comanche Street
Corpus Christi 78401
(512) 880-7000

DALLAS PUBLIC LIBRARY*+
Urban Information
1515 Young St.
Dallas 75201
(214) 670-1487

CENTER FOR VOLUNTEERISM &
NONPROFIT MANAGEMENT+
1918 Texas Avenue
El Paso 79901
(915) 532-5377

SOUTHWEST BORDER NONPROFIT
RESOURCE CENTER+
2412 South Closner
Edinburgh 78539
(956) 316-2610

FUNDING INFORMATION
CENTER*+
329 S. Henderson
Fort Worth 76104
(817) 334-0228

HOUSTON PUBLIC LIBRARY*+
Bibliographic Information Center
500 McKinney
Houston 77002
(713) 236-1313

LONGVIEW PUBLIC LIBRARY*
222 W. Cotton St.
Longview 75601
(903) 237-1352

LUBBOCK AREA FOUNDATION,
INC.*+
1655 Main St.
Suite 209
Lubbock 79401
(806) 762-8061

NONPROFIT RESOURCE CENTER OF
TEXAS*+
111 Soledad, Suite 200
San Antonio 78205
(210) 227-4333

WACO-McLENNAN COUNTY
LIBRARY*+
1717 Austin Ave.
Waco 76701
(254) 750-5975

NORTH TEXAS CENTER FOR
NONPROFIT MANAGEMENT*+
624 Indiana, Suite 307
Wichita Falls 76301
(817) 322-4961

UTAH

SALT LAKE CITY PUBLIC LIBRARY*
209 East 500 South
Salt Lake City 84111
(801) 524-8200

VERMONT

VERMONT DEPT. OF LIBRARIES*+
Reference & Law Info. Services
109 State St.
Montpelier 05609
(802) 828-3268

VIRGINIA

HAMPTON PUBLIC LIBRARY+
4207 Victoria Blvd.
Hampton 23669
(757) 727-1312

RICHMOND PUBLIC LIBRARY*+
Business, Science & Technology
101 East Franklin St.
Richmond 23219
(804) 780-8223

ROANOKE CITY PUBLIC LIBRARY
SYSTEM*
706 S. Jefferson
Roanoke 24016
(540) 853-2477

WASHINGTON

MID-COLUMBIA LIBRARY*
405 South Dayton
Kennewick 99336
(509) 586-3156

SEATTLE PUBLIC LIBRARY*+
Science, Social Science
1000 Fourth Ave.
Seattle 98104
(206) 386-4620

SPOKANE PUBLIC LIBRARY*
Funding Information Center
West 906 Main Ave.
Spokane 99201
(509) 626-5347

UNITED WAY OF PIERCE
COUNTY*+
Center for Nonprofit Development
1501 Pacific Ave., Suite 400
P.O. Box 2215
Tacoma 98401
(206) 272-4263

GREATER WENATCHEE
COMMUNITY FOUNDATION AT THE
WENATCHEE PUBLIC
LIBRARY
310 Douglas St.
Wenatchee 98807
(509) 662-5021

WEST VIRGINIA

KANAWHA COUNTY PUBLIC
LIBRARY*+
123 Capitol St.
Charleston 25301
(304) 343-4646

WISCONSIN

UNIVERSITY OF WISCONSIN-
MADISON*+
Memorial Library
728 State St.
Madison 53706
(608) 262-3242

MARQUETTE UNIVERSITY
MEMORIAL LIBRARY*+
Funding Information Center
1415 W. Wisconsin Ave.
Milwaukee 53233
(414) 288-1515

UNIVERSITY OF WISCONSIN-
STEVENS POINT*+
Library-Foundation Collection
99 Reserve St.
Stevens Point 54481-3897
(715) 346-4204

WYOMING

NATRONA COUNTY PUBLIC
LIBRARY*+
307 E. 2nd St.
Casper 82601-2598
(307) 237-4935

LARAMIE COUNTY COMMUNITY
COLLEGE*+
Instructional Resource Center
1400 E. College Dr.
Cheyenne 82007-3299
(307) 778-1206

CAMPBELL COUNTY PUBLIC
LIBRARY*+
2101 4-J Road
Gillette 82716
(307) 682-3223

TETON COUNTY LIBRARY*+
125 Virginian Lane
Jackson 83001
(307) 733-2164

ROCK SPRINGS LIBRARY+
400 C St.
Rock Springs 82901
(307) 362-6212

PUERTO RICO

UNIVERSIDAD DEL SAGRADO
CORAZON+
M.M.T. Guevara Library
Santurce 00914
(809) 728-1515 x 4357

All the indexes refer to the foundations by a four-digit number that appears above the foundation's name. As already mentioned, the foundations are arranged in alphabetical order according to the state in which they are incorporated.

Exhibit 7.5 shows a fictitious entry as it would appear in the *Foundation Directory.*

Exhibit 7.5

THE FOUNDATION DIRECTORY Sample Entry

2762
The Sebastian Jessica Foundation
2604 Northstar
Chicago 60604   (312) 896-8360
Incorporated in 1926 in IL.

Donor(s): Vastell Jessica, Mrs. Sebastian Jessica
Foundation type: Independent
Financial data (yr. ended 6/30/97): Assets, $150,444,176 (M); expenditures, $6,488,200; qualifying distributions, $6,400,200 including $4,488,200 for 126 grants (high: $300,000; low: $200; average: $10,000–$50,000). $85,200 for 65 employee matching gifts and $1,200,200 for 7 foundation administered programs.
Purpose and activities: Dedicated to enhancing the humane dimensions of life through activities that emphasize the theme of improving the quality of teaching and learning. Serves precollegiate education through grantmaking and program activities in elementary and secondary public education.
Fields of interest: Elementary and secondary public education, teaching, educational technology.
Types of support: Consulting services, technical assistance, special projects.
Limitations: No support for colleges and universities (except for projects in elementary and secondary education). No grants to individuals, or for building or endowment funds, or operating budgets; no loans.
Publications: Annual report, informational brochure (including application guidelines), financial statement, grants list.
Application information: Grant proposals for higher education not accepted; fellowship applications available only through participating universities.
Application form not required.
    Initial approach: letter
    Copies of proposal: 1
    Deadline(s): None
    Board meeting date(s): May and Nov., and as required
    Final notification: 4 weeks
    Write: Dr. Stefan Ross, Pres.
Officers: Vastell Jessica, Chair; Ann Jessica, Vice-Chair and Secy.; Stefan Ross, Pres.; Winifred L. Boser, V.P.; Franz Kirschbauer, Treas.; Bilal Ali, Prog. Dir.
Trustees: John R. Bige, Alice S. Romano, Donald C. Crowne, Jr., Charles Power, George Gaylin, P. John Passitty.
Number of staff: 4 full-time professionals; 1 part-time professional; 4 full-time support.
Employer Identification Number: 679014579

In an effort to find a funder for our example project involving parent, teacher, and student involvement through electronic interface, we turned to our key words and the subject index in the *Foundation Directory*. Using this resource, we were able to determine that the fictitious Jessica Foundation has expressed interest in elementary education and technology. From the entry we were also able to ascertain that our request will fall within the foundation's average grant size of $10,000 to $50,000. However, we are still not ready to write a proposal to them or even to telephone them.

We need to learn more about the foundation. What does it really value? What types of projects has it funded? And to what types of organizations did it make awards? As the *Foundation Directory* entry does not state that the foundation limits its giving to any one geographic area, we are also interested in knowing where they have awarded their past grants.

Another popular Foundation Center publication, the *Foundation Grants Index*, can provide us with much of this information. Published annually, it lists more than seventy-three thousand grants made by a thousand of the largest foundations. The 1998 edition indexes grant awards of $10,000 and larger. Grant descriptions are divided into broad subject areas. Within each, the grants are listed geographically by state and alphabetically by name. Because we know the Jessica Foundation is in Illinois and have the foundation name, the list of its grants can be easily located.

Exhibit 7.6 shows a fictitious example of an entry in Section I of the *Foundation Grants Index.*

Exhibit 7.6

THE FOUNDATION GRANTS INDEX Sample Entry

Education, Elementary and Secondary

The Sebastian Jessica Foundation

No support for colleges and universities (except for projects in elementary and secondary education). No grants to individuals or for building or endowment funds or operating budgets; no loans.

2713. Association of Indiana School Administrators, South Bend, IN. $25,000, 1997. For Reorganization of Schools Project through electronic interface. 9/14/97.

2714. Association of Michigan School Administrators, Detroit, MI. $14,000, 1997. For Consortium for Schools of the Future. 10/21/97.

2715. Hazelnut School District, Hazelnut, MO. $12,500, 1997. For Internet Homework Hotline Program. 7/9/97.

2716. Kids in Between, Kansas City, MO. $10,000, 1997. For educational technology program for teachers working with children and their parents. 10/15/97.

2717. Platterton School District, Agnes Middle School, Alexandria, VA. $13,000, 1997. For staff development activities related to improving student performance through technology. 7/15/97.

From this list, we can see that the Jessica Vastell Foundation appears to exhibit values commensurate with our project. It appears that a grant of $25,000 would be reaching the Foundation's upper limit and that a proposal for $10,000 to $15,000 might stand a better chance for funding. Chapter Eight provides you with more strategies for continuing your Values Approach to Grantseeking.

Besides having many excellent books on foundation funding, your Foundation Center Regional Library has three other references you should be familiar with.

- *990 Internal Revenue Service Foundation Tax Returns*—The IRS requires private foundations to file income tax returns each year. The 990–PF returns provide fiscal details on receipts and expenditures, compensation of officers, capital gains or losses, and other financial matters. Form 990–AR provides information on foundation managers, assets, and grants paid and committed for future payment. The Foundation Center's National Collection and field offices in New York City, San Francisco, Washington, D.C., Cleveland, and Atlanta have on microfiche the past three years of tax returns for all private foundations. Each Cooperating Collection has returns for private foundations located in its state and sometimes in surrounding states.

- *Grant Guides*—Published by the Foundation Center, these computer-produced guides to foundation giving are available in thirty-one subject areas. Each guide has three indexes—subject, geographic, and recipient.

- *FC Search*—This is the Foundation Center's database of forty-five thousand foundations and corporate givers on CD-ROM.

Corporate Research Tools

The current federal IRS rules allow a corporation to take up to 10 percent of its gross profits as a tax deduction when these profits are given as grants to nonprofit organizations—501(c)(3)s. However, I don't know of any corporations that give 10 percent. The national average is approximately 2 percent of gross profits.

In addition, not all corporate support takes the form of tax-deductible gifts. For example, when a corporation perceives that a potential grant project is blatantly self-serving (that is, enhances its marketplace positioning, product testing, or product development), it will often make the grant through its marketing department. This usually will not appear as a write-off against taxable profits and will not show up on any grant list. The inability to verify corporate support accounts for the inaccuracy and lack of specificity that characterize the corporate grants marketplace.

What motivates a corporation to make a grant? What benefits can they receive by funding you? Reviewing the values of corporate funders tells us that they are motivated by concern for their workers and the children of their workers, product development, and product positioning.

In the example project, the method of solution calls for the use of computers to provide a link between parent and teacher and between the student's level of performance and responsible educational practices. The project allows parents to review homework assignments and gain homework assistance through the Internet. Companies that have employees whose children attend the school may be interested; those that make, sell, or distribute computers and curriculum software may be interested even if they are outside the area. If the model project results in educational change such companies would benefit, because in addition to the benefits related directly to education, equipment and software producers also have the opportunity to position their products with parents and students—future consumers.

There are many reasons why companies support grant projects, but they are not simply interested in doing nice things for education. They want and expect a return on their investment.

How can you locate the companies that will be most interested in your project and its potential benefits? Your public library or local college library should have several helpful resources. In addition, if you are near a Foundation Center national collection or a regional cooperating collection, you have access to many resources, including two of the Foundation Center's primary corporate research tools:

- *The National Directory of Corporate Giving*—This provides information on over 1,905 corporate foundations and on an additional 990 direct corporate-giving programs. It also has an extensive bibliography and several indexes to help you target funding prospects.

- *Corporate Foundation Profiles*—This publication contains detailed analyses of 195 of the largest corporate foundations in the United States—grantmakers that each give $1.2 million or more annually.

Because companies define themselves in terms of markets and products, it would help you to look at those that might value your project because of its potential impact on their marketplace. The *Standard Industrial Classification Code Book,* available at your public library, is an excellent tool for finding out who makes what products. Once you have the names of the companies that manufacture the product you are interested in, you can telephone their local sales representatives or phone or write their corporate offices to find out their interest in your project.

One crucial fact to remember is that corporate grants decrease as profits go down. A look at *Dun and Bradstreet's Million Dollar Directory* will tell you the financial condition of America's largest businesses. If a company is paying its creditors late and owes money, it is not a prime target for a grant request.

Obtaining Grants from Companies in Your Community

Corporations in your area are your best bet for grant support. Start with companies near your school, where the children of the workers are served.

Although corporations give where they live, they also expect a professional approach. Many companies require that their employees be volunteers or members of the nonprofit organization's advisory group before they will award it grant support. And just as companies are judged by the quality of their sales representatives, your school will be judged by the quality of the individual chosen to approach the company. I recommend that you always check with a district administrator before you contact a company. You can get a grant. Many elementary and middle school teachers have personally taken their proposals to corporations and have been quite successful.

Chambers of Commerce usually print an annual listing of all the companies in their area. The listing ranks the companies by number of employees and payroll and often includes product information. It is an excellent grants research tool. Establish a Corporate Grants Advisory Group and invite several individuals from the corporate world to participate. One of them should be able to procure this invaluable list for you.

Because most corporations' grant money comes from their profits, knowing which local companies are profitable will be a big help. If you have a stockbroker on your Corporate Grants Advisory Group, ask the broker to find out which companies in your area are paying a stock dividend. In addition, companies are always concerned about their customers' credit ratings. How companies pay their bills is a reflection of their fiscal condition and profitability. Hence, companies subscribe to several services that help them keep close tabs on their customers. Ask the members of your Corporate Grants Advisory Group what services they use and if they could get you a credit report on the companies and corporations you are planning to approach.

Do not overlook smaller companies and independently owned businesses in your area. Individual companies or businesses may not be able to fund a grant idea on their own, but several could band together to fund a project. Just because a company or business does not employ hundreds of individuals does not mean it is not concerned about quality education. Like larger companies, smaller ones will expect to see a sound business plan as part of your proposal (more on this in Chapter Ten).

Other Research Tools

This chapter gives you information on materials that will help you in grantseeking. Many are inexpensive or can be used free. The bibliography notes even more resources. In addition to the tools mentioned, you may be interested in the many newsletters in the education and grants field. The following are those that I use in my work. I suggest that you contact the publisher for a free sample and subscription information: Capitol Publications, Inc., 1101 King Street, P.O. Box 1453, Alexandria, VA 22313-2053, 800-655-5597.

- *Education Daily*
- *Education Grants Alert*
- *Federal Grants and Contracts Weekly*
- *Foundation and Corporate Grants Alert*

Ready-Aim-Go to Chapter Eight to learn the basics on how to contact a grantor before you write your proposal. Do not make the novice's mistake of shotgunning your proposal to the list of grantors your research has uncovered. You increase your chances of success by a factor of five if you make preproposal contact.

Chapter 8

Contacting the Grantor Before You Write the Proposal

THIS CHAPTER MAY BE the most important one in the entire book. If you are thinking of skipping it, think again. It is estimated that contacting the grantor before you write your proposal increases your chances of success between 300 and 500 percent! Preproposal contact results in grants success because it allows you to gather the information you need to view your project through the values glasses of the potential funder. Nothing, except getting funded, is better than face-to-face contact with a grantor. In-person contact allows you to discuss with the funder several possible approaches to the problem and to ascertain the grantor's interest in your solutions.

I know what you're thinking now. You're thinking, Wait a minute! Writing a proposal is one thing, but making preproposal contact with a prospective grantor is more than can be expected from a full-time teacher. I hear you! But you need to know how dramatically preproposal contact can affect the outcome. Besides, you need not be the one who makes the contact. In fact, the best individual to make contact may be a volunteer. If you mobilized your grants effort through a grants advisory group, you may already have a volunteer with a sales and marketing background who would love to assist you. Contacting a funder will not cause a trained salesperson any anxiety. Remember, what is anxiety-producing for one person may not be for another. For example, your volunteer might find that facing your students for one day would be much more stressful than meeting face-to-face with a potential funding source.

I ask many grantseekers why they avoid preproposal contact. Their answers vary, but there is one consistent theme: they do not want to risk having their ideas rejected in a face-to-face meeting.

Whatever your reason, you must put it aside. Review your lists of connections and linkages for names of individuals who might be able to arrange preproposal contact with foundation or corporate board members, trustees, government bureaucrats, and so on. And remember, preproposal contact is not scary when you have done your homework and know enough about the prospective grantor to ask questions that reflect your knowledge rather than expose your ignorance.

First, review the Grantseekers' Decision Matrix (Table 6.1) to remind yourself of the values and interests of the *type* of funder you have decided to approach. Then review the research you have collected on each *specific* grantor. Naturally, any procedural requirements of a particular funding source should be followed. In general, however, you will find the following suggestions helpful.

How to Contact Foundation and Corporate Grantors

Many large foundations and corporations have Internet sites. You can print application forms when required off their websites or they will mail you general information concerning their grants program, including grant application guidelines, annual reports, and in a few cases newsletters. Use the Sample Letter to a Foundation or Corporation Requesting Information and Guidelines in Exhibit 8.1 as a guide for contacting *only* those that have stated, as found in your research, that application guidelines or other

---

Exhibit 8.1

SAMPLE LETTER TO A FOUNDATION OR CORPORATION REQUESTING INFORMATION AND GUIDELINES

Date

Name
Title
Address

Dear [Contact Person]:

My research on your [foundation/corporation] indicates that you provide application guidelines to prospective grantees. I am developing a proposal in the area of [topic] and I would appreciate receiving these guidelines at your earliest convenience.

I would also appreciate any other information you may have that could help us prepare a successful, quality proposal. Please add us to your mailing list for annual reports, newsletters, priority statements, program statements, and so on.

Since both of our organizations are committed to [subject area], I believe you will find our proposal idea of interest. [Mention any linkage or volunteer support relative to the foundation's or corporation's employees. Also, the linkage could jointly sign the letter or send it themselves.]

Sincerely,

Name/Title
Phone Number

information is available. Those foundations and corporations that provide guidelines usually have a director and a staff to respond to your request.

Please note that this is an inquiry letter for information only. It is *not* a proposal. Send this inquiry letter first, and if you get no response, you are justified in telephoning the foundation. The majority of these private grantors have no application guidelines and state "no contact except by letter." In these cases you must submit a letter proposal (see Chapter Thirteen).

Telephoning Foundations and Corporations

Fewer than a thousand of the forty thousand foundations have offices. Therefore, telephone contact is limited. Many entries in foundation resource directories do not list telephone numbers. Even if it is listed in an entry or on an IRS tax return, do not call if the information clearly states that there should be no contact except by letter.

Corporations usually have staff assigned to their corporate giving programs. They value their time highly and allocate it to making money—not giving it away. With larger grantors it is proper to send a letter first. Then telephone if you do not get a response.

In general, if you have a phone number for a foundation or corporation and you are not aware of any rules or instructions that discourage phone contact, you *should* telephone them. Of course, the optimum approach is to arrange a personal visit. If a face-to-face meeting is not possible, try to gather the same information you would in a visit via the telephone.

E-mail or fax it! The 1990s have added a new dimension to preproposal contact. When you talk to the foundation or corporate official to discuss your approaches to solving the problem, ask if you can e-mail or fax her or him a one-page summary of your ideas, and call back to discuss the ideas. Try to arrange a mutually agreeable time to talk.

Steps for Contacting Foundations and Corporations

First, if appropriate, phone the contact person. Your purpose for calling is to validate the information you have already collected. Your questions should reflect your knowledge concerning the foundation's or corporation's granting pattern and priorities and elicit their interest in your approaches to solving a problem or increasing educational opportunities for students. Introduce yourself and state the purpose of the call. (You may find it helpful to review your needs data before calling.) Remember, you are not calling for yourself but for your students, your school, and the field of education. If you reach a secretary or administrative assistant, ask to talk to the foundation director, corporate contributions officer, or staff person best able to answer your questions.

Second, demonstrate that you are different from other grantseekers. Show that you have purposefully selected the foundation or corporation by asking a question that reflects your research. For example, "I am contacting the _____ Foundation [Corporation] because you have demonstrated a desire to _____. My research shows that 40 percent of your funds in recent years were committed to this area."

Third, explain what you want. For example, "I would appreciate five minutes of your time to ascertain which of the approaches I have developed for the XYZ School would appeal to your board and elicit your foundation's greatest support." You might use the fax approach here to maintain their interest.

Remember, you are presenting the funder with an opportunity to meet its needs. You are not begging. Funders are looking for good programs to support, so get them excited about yours!

Fourth, try to arrange a meeting. You would be happy to go to the funder, or it may be interested in sending a representative to visit you at your school; a visitor could observe your students and see the needs population or problem firsthand. You would be happy either way. The funder will expect to pay its way to visit you and you to pay your way to visit it.

Fifth, decide who should represent you. Whether you visit the funder or the funder comes to you, your team should be small, usually no larger than two. Select an active and concerned volunteer from your grants advisory group who is donating time to your proposed project. The other person may be yourself or another paid professional.

A few words about what to wear: the rule of thumb is to dress the way the foundation official dresses. Although many from the world of education are offended by the notion that people are judged by how they dress, it is worthwhile to take a look at *Dress for Success* by John T. Malloy. You may be surprised to learn that Malloy's original work was funded by a grant. His project was designed to test whether a classroom leader's way of dressing has an impact on students' learning and retention. He found that it does. Very few educators ever read the research findings or improved their dress habits because of them, but corporations picked up on Malloy's findings. In short, you are judged by what you wear, so dress accordingly. Your project and students are worth your best effort to project a good image to the prospective funding source. But don't go overboard. Wear clothes you are comfortable in.

Sixth, decide what should be taken to the meeting. What you take is extremely important. Focus on your objective. What do you expect to accomplish in a person-to-person visit with the potential grantor? You want the following:

- Agreement on the need or problem to be addressed

- A discussion of the prospective funder's interest in your proposed solution

- Information on the grants decision process so you can tailor your approach

- Validation of your research and estimate on the amount of your grant request

Avoid the common mistake of jumping directly to the money issue by concentrating on bringing material that solidifies agreement on the need or the problem. In many cases, the grantor has difficulty seeing the problem through the eyes of a student or educator. Use the following techniques to help the funder develop insight into the problem.

- *Videotapes:* Make a short (three- to five-minute) videotape that demonstrates the problem. A student-made tape can be very moving. Students can make a short video as a class or school project. Whether it deals with alcohol abuse or zoology, a short video tells a compelling story because it enables the funder to *see* what the need is.

- *Slides and Audiotapes:* As an example, I once had my students develop a five-minute slide presentation on alcohol use and abuse as a basis for a parent-child prevention program. We did not even have a machine that changed the slides automatically. We simply made an audiotape that played on a battery-operated cassette player that was started at the same time as the slide projector, set on three-second delay. The narrator was a volunteer from my Parent Advisory Group who just happened to be a former radio announcer. Needless to say, the grantor was very impressed that this professional-looking and -sounding program was done by students and volunteers at a cost of less than $10!

- *Picture Book:* A picture book that documents the need may provide the starting point for a discussion of how the funder views the problem.

Your materials should be aimed at educating the grantor, not convincing it. Again, the objective of the meeting is to establish agreement on the need for a project and then to ascertain the funding source's interests and to discuss several approaches or solutions to the problem.

Recording Your Research and Preproposal Contact

One reason for preproposal contact is to validate your research on the funding source and to add to that body of knowledge so that you can develop a grant-winning strategy. You want your research to be organized and to take advantage of every possible timesaving technique.

If you haven't already done so, establish a file for each grantor you are thinking about approaching. Keep the files together in alphabetical order. This will be a great start in organizing your grants effort.

Generate Foundation or Corporation Research Worksheets (Exhibit 8.2) for the grantors you believe are your most likely prospects for funding, based on your research. Use each worksheet to keep a record of the information you have gathered to date. Update the worksheet as you obtain additional information and materials. Also use the worksheet to log all contact made with the foundation or corporation, including face-to-face, telephone, and written contact.

In addition to information on a particular foundation, it is also important to collect as much information as you can on individual foundation officers, board members, and trustees. This information can help you determine ways to deal with any preferences and biases you may encounter and to locate other possible linkages between the foundation, your school, a volunteer on your Grants Advisory Group, and so on.

Use the Foundation or Corporation Funding Staff History Worksheet (Exhibit 8.3) to record the information you collect. Store the worksheet in the appropriate foundation's file.

How to Contact Government Grantors

Contact with government agencies is encouraged by letter, phone, and, when possible, in person. The first step is to send the agency a letter requesting program information and to be put on the agency's mailing list. Use the Sample Letter to a Federal Agency Requesting Information and Guidelines (Exhibit 8.4) when appropriate.

Second, telephone the federal agency that you have discovered in your search. The *Catalog of Federal Domestic Assistance* may provide you with an individual's name as well as with the agency's phone number and e-mail. Have at hand the name of the informational contact you developed from your research, but don't be surprised if the person listed in your research transferred to another agency or is not the best individual to assist you.

Inform the person who answers the phone that you are calling for information concerning one of the agency's grant programs and give the CFDA reference number and the name of the program. It usually takes one or two referrals to get the correct person and program. Introduce

Exhibit 8.2

FOUNDATION OR CORPORATION RESEARCH WORKSHEET

Foundation or Corporation: _____

Create a file for each foundation you are researching and place all the information you gather on this foundation in the file. Use the Foundation Research Worksheet to do the following:

- Keep a record of the information you have gathered
- Maintain a log of all telephone and face-to-face contact with the foundation/corporation
- Log all correspondence sent to and received from the foundation/corporation

Address: _____   Name of Contact Person: _____

Telephone Number: _____   Title of Contact Person: _____

Fax Number: _____

Place a check mark (✔) next to the information you have gathered and put in the file for the foundation/corporation.

_____ Description of the granting program

      Source: _____

_____ Information on past grants

      Source: _____

_____ Application information/guidelines

      _____ Sent for   _____ Received

_____ Annual Report

      _____ Sent for   _____ Received

_____ Newsletter/other reports

      _____ Sent for   _____ Received

_____ Funding staff history   _____ IRS form 990 (fdn. only)

_____ Written summary of each contact made   _____ Financial/profit statements (corp. only)

_____ Grantor Strategy Worksheet   _____ Chamber of Commerce data (corp. only)

_____ List of board members/officers   _____ Product information/SIC code (corp. only)

Record of Face-to-Face and Telephone Contact:

Date Contacted	Contacted by	Foundation Contact	Results	Action

Record of All Correspondence Sent and Received:

Date of Correspondence	Purpose of Correspondence	Results/Action

Exhibit 8.3

FOUNDATION OR CORPORATION FUNDING STAFF HISTORY WORKSHEET

Foundation or Corporation: _____

1. Name of director/contributions officer: _____

2. Title: _____

3. Residence address: _____ Phone: _____

4. Business address: _____ Phone: _____

5. Linkages/contacts (mutual friends/associates who can contact director/contributions officer for you):

_____

_____

_____

_____

List any data you have uncovered that might help you:

- Determine ways to deal with any of contact's preferences and biases
- Locate other possible linkages between this individual and you/your school's volunteer on your Grants Advisory Group, etc.

6. Birthdate: _____ Birthplace:_____

7. Marital status: _____ Children: _____

8. Employer: _____ Job title: _____

9. College/university:_____ Degree(s): _____

10. Military service: _____

11. Clubs/affiliations: _____

12. Interests/hobbies: _____

13. Other board memberships: _____

14. Other philanthropic activities: _____

15. Awards/honors: _____

16. Other: _____

Notes:

Exhibit 8.4

SAMPLE LETTER TO A FEDERAL AGENCY REQUESTING INFORMATION AND GUIDELINES

Date

Name

Title

Address

Dear [Contact Person]:

I am interested in the grant opportunities under [CFDA #], [Program Title]. Please add my name to your mailing list to receive information on this program. I am particularly interested in receiving application forms, program guidelines, and any existing priorities statements.

Please also send any other information that could help me prepare a quality application, such as a list of last year's successful grant recipients and reviewers. I am enclosing a self-addressed envelope for your convenience in sending these lists.

I will be contacting you when it is appropriate to discuss my proposal ideas. Thank you for your assistance.

Sincerely,
Name/Title
Phone Number

---

yourself and ask to speak with the program officer or with someone who can answer a few brief but important questions.

Third, demonstrate your knowledge, not your ignorance. Your research has provided you with a considerable amount of information. Use this opportunity to validate it. Check the accuracy of the deadline dates and appropriations printed in the CFDA.

Fourth, tell contacts what you want! Ask for a few minutes of their time. These are government employees; there is more support staff involved in the government grants process than the foundation or corporate, and Freedom of Information rules must be observed in tax-supported grantseeking. Staff members are generally helpful and willing, if not eager, to provide information.

Your objective is to discuss your approaches to solving the problem. Some federal programs actually request a preproposal meeting or submission of a concept paper. Believe it or not, they want you to submit the best possible proposal, even if they are unable to fund it. The better your proposal and the more requests they receive, the more their program is needed.

If you cannot visit the federal agency in Washington, D.C., and do not have a volunteer who can visit for you, a phone conversation is your first alternative. E-mail may also work. Again, ask permission to fax or e-mail a one-page concept paper and to call after the agency representative has had time to review it. Ask the contact person to place you on the agency's mailing list to receive guidelines, application information, newsletters, and so on.

Review the diagram of the Proactive Grantseekers' $85 Billion Federal Grants Clock in Figure 8.1 and ask where the agency is in the grants process.

Ask if the agency has published anything in the *Federal Register* about its grantmaking rules. If so, ask for the date of publication and the page number. Also request a list of last year's grantees (it may be through the Internet, but if you cannot find it, ask the grantor how to locate it or ask that a copy be sent to you). The list tells you who got how much grant money and will help you determine if your school or community stands a chance of receiving funds or if you would be better off developing a consortium with other districts, joining with your intermediate district, or becoming part of a college or university's grant.

Ask the agency official for information on the agency's peer review system. The *Federal Register* may have information on the points that the

Figure 8.1

THE PROACTIVE GRANTSEEKER'S $85 BILLION FEDERAL GRANTS CLOCK

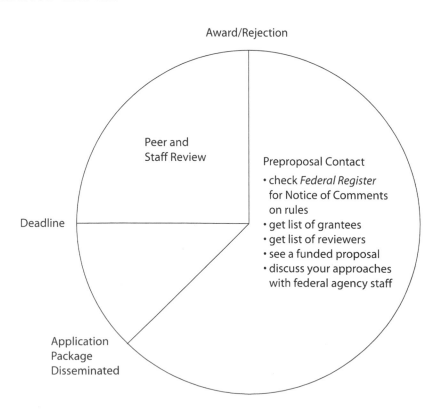

reviewers award for each section of a proposal, but you need to know who reads the grant applications. Request a list of last year's reviewers. Knowing the types of reviewers and their background will help you determine what writing style to use and how to construct your proposal. In addition, ask the program officer how you could become a reviewer so you can learn more about the review process.

You may also ask the program officer what educational conferences or professional meetings she or he is planning to attend in the near future. You may be able to meet with the official at a meeting near your school.

Sixth, decide who should represent you at the meeting. You could send a volunteer from your grants advisory group. Of course, the best approach would be for you to go with the volunteer. Two is the magic number when it comes to representation. If you send more, the federal program officer will begin to wonder who is back home teaching!

In matters of dress, federal program officers are usually quite conservative. But there is a difference between the Department of Education and the National Endowment for the Humanities. Program officers usually dress more casually in the arts and humanities than in education and science. Dress as much like the program officer as possible. The older the bureaucrat, the more conservative the dress. Malloy's book *Dress for Success* has a section on how to dress for meetings with government bureaucrats.

Seventh, decide what you or your representatives should take to the meeting. Take materials that help demonstrate the need. These may include audiovisual aids such as short (three- to five-minute) filmstrips, videotapes, slide presentations, pictures, and so on. In addition, representatives may leave information on your community, school district, school, or classroom with the official. But *never* leave a proposal.

Your representatives may also want to have with them, or better yet, commit to memory, a list of questions to ask the program officer.

Recording Federal Research and Preproposal Contact

Keep copies of the information you gather on a prospective government funding source and record all contacts and correspondence on the Federal Research Worksheet in Exhibit 8.5. Record all information you gather on agency personnel on the Federal Funding Staff History Worksheet (Exhibit 8.6).

The Grantor Strategy Worksheet

Complete a Grantor Strategy Worksheet (Exhibit 8.7) for each funding source you plan to submit a proposal to. This worksheet also helps you understand the funder's point of view.

Exhibit 8.5

FEDERAL RESEARCH WORKSHEET

CFDA No. _____   Deadline Date(s): _____

Program Title: _____   Gov't. Agency: _____

Create a file for each program you are researching and place all the information you gather on this program in the file. Use this Federal Research Worksheet to:

- Keep a record of the information you have gathered
- Maintain a log of all telephone and face-to-face contacts made with the government agency
- Log all correspondence sent to and received from the agency

Agency Address: _____   Agency Director: _____

Telephone Number: _____   Program Director: _____

Fax Number: _____   Name/Title of Contact Person: _____

Place a check mark (✔) next to the information you have gathered and placed in the file for the foundation.

_____ Program description from CFDA   _____ Notice of rules for evaluation from
_____ Letter requesting to be put on mailing list   *Federal Register*
    _____ Sent for _____ Received   _____ Grant scoring system—point allocation
_____ List of last year's grantees   for each section. Source:
    _____ Sent for _____ Received   _____
_____ List of last year's reviewers   _____ Sample funded proposal
    _____ Sent for _____ Received   _____ Federal Funding Staff History Worksheet
_____ Application package—expected availability date   _____ Written summary of each contact made
    _____ Sent for _____ Received   _____ Grantor Strategy Worksheet
_____ Comments on rules/final rules from *Federal Register*

Record of Face-to-Face and Telephone Contact:

Date Contacted	Contacted by	Foundation Contact	Results	Action

Record of All Correspondence Sent and Received:

Date of Correspondence	Purpose of Correspondence	Results/Action

---

Exhibit 8.6

FEDERAL FUNDING STAFF HISTORY WORKSHEET

CFDA No. _____

Program Title: _____

Gov't. Agency: _____

1. Name: _____

2. Title: _____
       (Agency Director, Program Director, Program Officer, etc.)

3. Business address: _____

4. Business telephone: _____

5. Birthdate: _____   Birthplace: _____

6. Marital status: _____   Children: _____

7. College/university _____

8. Degree(s): _____

9. Military service: _____

10. Clubs/affiliations: _____

11. Interests/hobbies: _____

12. Board memberships: _____

13. Other philanthropic activities: _____

14. Awards/honors: _____

15. Other: _____

Notes:

Take full advantage of your ability to analyze the funding source's granting history. Even if you have not been able to make preproposal contact, it is imperative that the amount you are requesting fits the funding source's granting pattern.

Think about whom you might collaborate with on your proposal and what group might better serve as the submitting organization.

Make every attempt to find out *who* will be reading and evaluating your proposal. For example, will your proposal be read by staff members? board members? program personnel? outside experts or reviewers? This

Exhibit 8.7

GRANTOR STRATEGY WORKSHEET

Potential Grantor: _____   **Priority #:** _____

Deadline: _____

A.   Strategy Derived from Granting Pattern

    1. $_____   Largest grant to organization most similar to ours

    2. $_____   Smallest grant to organization most similar to ours

    3. $_____   Average grant size to organizations similar to ours

    4. $_____   Average grant size in our area of interest

    5. $_____   Our estimated grant request

    6.   Financial trend in our area of interest over past three years

        _____ Up   _____ Down   _____ Stable

    7.   If your proposal is a multiyear proposal, how popular have these been with the funding source in the past three years?

        _____ Many multiyear proposals funded

        _____ Some multiyear proposals funded

        _____ Few multiyear proposals funded

        _____ No multiyear funding

        _____ Not applicable

    8.   Financial data on funding source: obligation levels for last three years for grants

        19_____ $_____   19_____ $_____   19_____ $_____

B.   Based on preproposal contact, which solution strategies are the most appropriate for this funding source?

C.   Proposal Review System

    1.   Who evaluates submitted proposals? _____

        _____

    2.   What is the background and training of the evaluators? _____

        _____

        _____

    3.   What point system will be followed?_____

        _____

        _____

    4.   How much time will be spent reviewing each proposal? _____

        _____

D.   Use this space to note anything special that will affect proposal outcome.

_____

_____

_____

_____

information not only helps you write your proposal, it is also vital to performing a mock review, which will be discussed in Chapter Twelve.

Rank the funding sources that represent your best prospects. Eventually, you will tailor your proposal to those at the top of the list.

You probably will be missing some vital pieces of information. But based on what you have, devise the best strategy you can, and go for it! Once you have determined your strategy, go on to Chapter Nine to learn how to develop objectives.

Chapter 9

Developing Project Objectives

THROUGH PREPROPOSAL CONTACT, you determine which of your solutions appeals most to the prospective grantor. This helps you decide which solution to propose. If you are unable to make preproposal contact, use your list of grantees and reviewers to help you make the best choice. Once you have selected the best solution or approach, you must develop your proposal objectives. An objective is a measurable step taken to narrow or close the gap between what is and what ought to be. A well-constructed objective tells the funding source what will change as a result of the funds they provide.

Many grantseekers do not understand the difference between an objective and a method. Some actually write objectives that focus on the approaches or methods that will be used to bring about the change. This confuses *what* will be accomplished with *how* it will be accomplished.

To be sure you develop a well-constructed objective, ask yourself if there is more than one way to reach it. If there is only one possible approach, then you are dealing with a solution, not an objective. By asking yourself why you are performing a particular activity, you may back into your objective. In doing so, you will strengthen your proposal and develop a clear sense of what you should measure as you close the gap in the area of need.

An objective provides a measurable way to see how much change will occur by the conclusion of the project. A method tells *how* this change will be accomplished. A simple rule of thumb is this:

Objectives tell what you want to accomplish, and methods tell how you will accomplish it.

Developing objectives may seem tedious, especially when you are eager to write your proposal. But keep in mind that well-written objectives that focus on the measurable change to be accomplished will make your proposal more interesting and compelling to the funder and will enable you to measure the changes the proposal suggests.

In addition, when writing a proposal, most grantseekers want to move quickly to how they will do their project instead of first presenting what is to be accomplished. Measurement and evaluation to these grantseekers often focus on such issues as how many students will be exposed to a new piece of equipment or teaching regime rather than what the students will be able to do as a result of the experience. Well-written objectives help combat this problem.

This guide outlines a process for developing well-constructed objectives, but the ultimate judge is the grantor. There are vast differences in the ways grantors prefer objectives to be written. By procuring a copy of a funded proposal and discussing your proposal idea with the funding source prior to submission, you will obtain a much more accurate idea of what it considers a good objective and therefore have a better chance of winning support.

If you are unable to obtain a funded proposal or make preproposal contact to discuss your approach, the Objectives Worksheet (Exhibit 9.1) and the following guidelines for developing objectives provide a secure basis for organizing your approach. In general, a good objective has an action verb and a statement, a measurement indicator, a performance standard, a deadline, and a cost frame.

Action Verb and Statement

These describe what will change if your project is completed successfully. First review your Needs Worksheet (Exhibit 4.1) and Goals Worksheet (Exhibit 4.3). Remember, you are not suggesting or promising that the goal will be met and the gap entirely eliminated, only that a measurable part of it will be closed through the grant and the successful completion of your prescribed actions. Do not worry about being uncertain whether your proposed solution, model project, or research proposal will be 100 percent successful. You are proposing a solution, and even if it is unsuccessful, the field of education will learn from the experience.

For instance, in the example of the project to promote educationally responsible behavior in parents, teachers, and students, it is unlikely that the proposed approach will close the gap entirely. But we can't measure what we can't state! Put simply, the project will increase educationally responsible behavior in parents, teachers, and students—which does not mean it will eradicate irresponsible behavior.

As a professional educator, you probably studied how to construct behavioral objectives in college. You may now find it helpful to retrieve

Exhibit 9.1

OBJECTIVES WORKSHEET

Review your Needs and Goals Worksheets from Chapter Four. This will help you develop objectives that take demonstrable steps to close the gap between what exists now and what should be. If you are able to study a copy of a funded proposal, take note of the way the objectives are constructed. Always defer to the grantor's guidelines or the example provided by successful proposals. When in doubt, or when lacking information, use the following format to help you construct winning objectives.

Format: To [action verb and statement] by [performance standard] as measured by [measurement indicator] by [time] at a cost of $[cost].

Example: To increase completion rates in Smith Elementary School by 50 percent, as measured by the Smith School Completion Rate, in one year, at a cost of $20,000.

1.   In what area do you expect to see change as a result of the successful completion of your methods? (Example: completion rates)

2.   How much change (performance standard) do you forecast as an index of your success? (Example: 50% increase in completion rates)

3.   What measurement indicator will you use to denote the change? (Example: Smith School Completion Rate)

4.   How long will it take to implement your proposal and measure the change? (Example: one year)

5.   How much will it cost to accomplish your objective? (Example: $20,000)

the appropriate texts from your bookshelf. For instance, *Taxonomy of Educational Objectives, Handbook I: The Cognitive Domain* will help you develop knowledge-centered objectives, and *Handbook II: The Affective Domain* will help you develop values-centered objectives.

When you ask what will change as a result of your project, you may find that some of your answers fall in the realm of knowledge and others in the realm of values and feelings. In the example concerning educationally responsible behavior, some outcomes might be cognitive and others affective, which means that you would attempt to develop behavior that reflects both knowledge and appreciation of the value of education.

Measurement Indicator

This describes how you will measure the area you are attempting to change. Just as there are many ways to accomplish objectives, there are often several strategies that can measure change in your area of need. Begin by asking what students would do differently after you provide them with your solution or method of solving the problem.

Cognitive skills are usually the easiest to measure. In many cases, tests for this purpose already exist. For instance, there are standardized tests that can measure an increase in reading ability. If there is not a test available, you can always include the task of developing one in your proposal.

Literacy rates can be easily measured, as can computer literacy, math skills, and so on. But how do we measure values? To determine how to measure values, feelings, or attitudes, ask yourself how an individual would act who already values the desired outcome. For example, if the desired outcome of a project is to instill an appreciation for Elizabethan literature, you would ask how a student who already values Elizabethan literature acts. You may decide that students who truly like Elizabethan literature read it for their own satisfaction and not just to fulfill an assignment. If this is the case, you could add a component to your project that calls for placing several works of Elizabethan literature in the school library and then keeping a record of their use. If your project deals with performing arts, you might consider measuring appreciation by the number of students who attend a performance on their own, sign up for the school band, volunteer to work on the class play, and so on.

In one proposal I worked on, the objective was to increase teenagers' sense of responsibility toward alcohol consumption. Once the activities and methods were chosen, I was responsible for determining how the outcome would be measured. I decided that we would analyze certain pre- and postproject statistics, such as the number of alcohol-related deaths and accidents and of driving-while-intoxicated (DWI) charges. We would also administer a pre- and posttest to measure attitudinal changes concerning the subject. I developed a Responsible Drinking Scale and evaluated the responses to this survey in conjunction with statistics taken from police records.

In the project to increase educationally responsible behavior, we can measure the closing of the gap between what exists now and what ought to be in a variety of ways. For instance, we could look for behavior we believe indicates a developing sense of responsibility in the educational process: improved grades, less absenteeism, more students successfully completing their grade, more time spent on homework, more teacher-parent contacts, more parent-child discussions about education, and fewer hours spent watching television. We might even develop an Educational Responsibility Scale that contains questions aimed at surveying many of these points.

Performance Standard

This is the amount of change necessary to consider the project successful. A grantor will look at your objectives, make note of the amount you are requesting, examine your measurement indicators, and compare the amount of your request with the expected amount of change.

For example, if a project proposes to increase the reading scores of a certain target population from the 50th to the 70th percentile as measured by the Flockmeister Reading Scale, the percentile increase needs to be justified according to the number and type of students in the target population, the cost per student, and the long-term effects of such an increase.

If that increase can be correlated to an increase in the likelihood of students graduating from grade school, junior high, and eventually high school and can be brought about at a cost of $100 per student rather than $1,000, the grantor is likely to think the percentile increase very meaningful.

In the sample project to increase responsible educational behavior, we might be able to show a percentage increase by developing a scale that would survey several of the behavioral indicators previously mentioned. Thus far the objective might look something like this:

To increase the responsible educational behavior of parents, students, and teachers in the XYZ Elementary School [action verb and statement] by 25 percent [performance standard], as measured by the Responsible Education Scale [measurement indicator].

Deadline

This indicates the time needed to accomplish the desired degree of change. When you deal with government grants this is usually decided for you: most such grants are for one year. This is because of the way the budget appropriation cycle operates. However, there is currently a movement to allow multiyear awards because it is difficult to create the behavioral change outlined in an objective in just twelve months; it may take a good part of that time just to develop and conduct a pretest that provides the baseline data for the posttest.

In dealing with a multiyear project, you may want to create your objective with a one-year goal for change and increase the change indicated in the measurement indicator over subsequent years. For example, in the educationally responsible behavior project, the objective could indicate a 25 percent increase in year one and a 40 percent increase by the end of year two.

Cost

Include the cost of accomplishing the change in the body of your objective. This provides a stark reminder of how much it costs to accomplish change. It also demonstrates that you have a total command of your proposal. You know what will be accomplished, how much will be accomplished, and what it will cost.

However, in most cases you cannot include cost in an objective until you have completed your budget. The Project Planner in Chapter Ten helps you develop a budget that shows the cost of each objective. Once you have completed your Project Planner, go back to your objectives and add a cost component to each.

To determine the cost of developing change more accurately, divide the total cost of the project by the number of students it will serve. This gives you the cost per student served. If it seems high, ask yourself how many students will benefit in future years and how many students at other schools will benefit once you disseminate your information to them. Proposals that contain equipment may seem excessively expensive, particularly when you think in terms of only one classroom. But when you take into consideration that the equipment will be used for five years and shared with other classrooms, the cost per student served seems much more acceptable.

In the 1970s many demonstration models were developed that never could be replicated because the cost per person served was excessive. Funding sources are trying not to repeat this mistake. By keeping your eye on the cost of accomplishing your objectives and creating the change you desire, you can keep education grounded in economic reality.

Chapter 10

Building a Project Planner

ONLY AFTER YOU HAVE UNCOVERED as much information about the prospective grantor as you can and completed a Grantor Strategy Worksheet (Exhibit 8.7) should you begin to finalize your project design. Ideally, you will have already presented the prospective grantor with several interesting alternatives and explored the grantor's interest in your project and the amount of investment it is ready to make. Many grantseekers make the mistake of writing their proposals first, before they look for grantors. This not only limits the number of potential grantors, but usually indicates reluctance to change approaches or project designs to accommodate funders once the proposal has been written.

Even if you are unable to use the preproposal contact strategies in Chapter Eight, you must choose the solution or approach that is most likely to offer the prospective grantor what it wants. Your research should have at least uncovered the funder's range of grant awards. If your proposal requires more funds than a single grantor is likely to invest, you need a project plan that specifies the funds you are requesting from each funder and shows what parts of your project each grantor will fund.

The Values-Based Approach to Grantseeking requires that you view your proposal through the eyes of the funder and that you provide each with a plan tailored to its needs. The funder may not see the methods, budget, or grant request the same way you do, and each type of grantor views these issues differently. For example, government grantors prefer well-organized proposals that allow them to easily identify matching or in-kind contributions and may require a budget narrative that links each expenditure to a method. Most corporate and foundation funders operate under an entirely different set of expectations. They often apply a business approach to their grant decision making and cost analysis.

Irrespective of the type of funding source, all grantors require that you have a plan. Just as you require student teachers to have a well-developed lesson plan before you give them access to your pupils and classroom, funding sources require grantees to have a well-developed plan before they give them access to their funds. The Project Planner in Exhibit 10.1 provides for this.

Think of the Project Planner as your lesson plan. Write the plan when you have a good idea of the preferred solution, who your key staff will be, your consortium arrangements, and the matching or in-kind contributions you will have.

The Project Planner helps you to develop a clearly defined proposal methodology and to conceptualize your grant plan and budget. Once completed, it allows you to define and refine several aspects of your project:

1. An adequate staffing pattern that describes who is needed to do what tasks when (to help ensure that your job descriptions match the tasks that need to be accomplished)

2. An easily scanned overview of the prescribed activities and how they relate to cost and the attainment of the objectives

3. A logical framework in which to evaluate the tasks performed by consultants

4. A detailed analysis of the materials, supplies, and equipment related to each objective

5. A defensible budget and cash forecast

6. An efficient way to document your in-kind or matching component

The Project Planner will appeal most to those funding sources that are familiar with and use spreadsheet formulas. It is a particularly effective tool in government proposals. Today more than ever federal program officers push grantees to carry out their entire proposals as presented for amounts less than requested. Because federal budget forms use broad budget categories, it is difficult to negotiate final awards. Standard federal budget forms make it difficult to demonstrate to the funder how a reduction in funds will have an impact on a specific objective. By using the Project Planner, the grantee can show this and demonstrate how it will affect the ability to achieve the proposal's objectives and ultimately the ability to bring about the desired change. The Project Planner allows you to present a clear picture of the relationship between project personnel, consultants, equipment and supplies, and the accomplishment of your proposal.

Completing a Project Planner

The following general guidelines follow the format of the planner sample shown in Exhibit 10.1.

Exhibit 10.1

PROJECT PLANNER

PROJECT PLANNER

PROJECT TITLE: _____

Proposal Developed for: _____

Project Director: _____

Proposed Start Date _____

Proposal Year _____

A. List project objectives or outcomes A. B.
B. List methods to accomplish each objective as A-1, A-2, ... B-1, B-2 ...

MONTH		TIME	PROJECT PERSONNEL	PERSONNEL COSTS			CONSULTANTS CONTRACT SERVICES				NON-PERSONNEL RESOURCES NEEDED SUPPLIES - EQUIPMENT - MATERIALS				SUB-TOTAL ACTIVITY COST	MILESTONES PROGRESS INDICATORS		
Begin	End			Salaries & Wages	Fringe Benefits	Total	Time	Cost/Week	Total		Item	Cost/Item	Quantity	Tot cost	Total I, L, P	Item		Date
C/D		E	F	G	H	I	J	K	L		M	N	O	P	Q	R		S

Total Direct Costs or Costs Requested From Funder

Matching Funds, In-Kind Contributions, or Donated Costs

Total Costs

Total I, L, P ___ T

% of Total ___ 100%

©David G. Bauer Associates, Inc.
(800) 836-0732

Objectives and Methods

In the column labeled A/B, list your project objectives and label each—for example, Objective A, Objective B, Objective C, and so on. Under each, list the methods you will use to accomplish each of the objectives. Think of the methods as the tasks or activities you will use to meet the need. Label each of the methods under its appropriate objective. For example, A–1, B–1, C–1, and so on.

Month

In column C/D, record the month you will begin each activity or task and the month you will end each. Writing 1/4, for example, means you intend to begin the first month after you receive funding and carry out the activities over four months (sixteen weeks). If you know the expected start-up month, note it here.

Time

In column E, record the number of person hours, weeks, or months needed to accomplish each task listed in Column A/B.

Project Personnel

In column F, list the names of key personnel who will spend a measurable or significant amount of time on each task or activity listed and on each objective. (You have already recorded the amount of time in Column E.)

Personnel Costs

In the next three columns, list the salaries and wages (column G), fringe benefits (column H), and total compensation (column I) for each of the key personnel listed in column F.

Start by coming up with rough job descriptions by listing the activities each person will be responsible for and the minimum qualifications you require. Determine whether each will be full- or part-time by looking at the number of hours, weeks, or months they will be needed. Once you have developed a rough job description, you can call a placement agency to get an estimate of the salary needed to fill the position.

Be sure to include services from your organization that will be donated. Put an asterisk next to all donated personnel and remember that their fringes as well as their wages will be donated. Identifying donated personnel is crucial when matching or in-kind contributions are required, and may be advantageous even if not; matching contributions show good faith and make you seem a better investment. Indeed, put an asterisk by *any-thing* donated (such as supplies, equipment, and materials) as you complete the remaining columns.

Consultants and Contract Services

In the next three columns, list the time (column J), cost per week (column K), and total cost (column L) of assistance to be provided by consultants and other contractors. These are individuals not in your normal employ who provide services not normally provided by someone in your organization. (Note: no fringe benefits are paid to these.)

Nonpersonnel Resources Needed: Supplies, Equipment, Materials

Use the next four columns to list the supplies, equipment, and materials needed to complete each activity and itemize the associated costs. In column M, list the items; in column N, list the cost per item; in column O list the quantity of each item; and in column P list the total cost.

Do not underestimate the resources needed to achieve your objectives. Ask yourself and your key personnel what is needed to complete each activity. Again, designate donated items with an asterisk.

Subtotal Cost for Activity

Add columns I, L, and P—the totals of personnel costs, consultants and contract services, and nonpersonnel resources—and note the sum in column Q. You can do this either for each activity or for each objective. If you do it by objective, you will have to add the subtotals for all the activities that fall under the objective.

Milestones and Progress Indicators

In column R, list what you will show the funding source to tell them how you are working toward accomplishing your objectives (such as a quarterly report). Think of these as milestones or progress indicators. In column S, record the dates by which the funding source will receive the listed milestones or progress indicators.

There are many ways to complete the Project Planner. The key is to make sure it works for *you* as you plan and implement your proposal. It will help you develop a clear picture of the personnel, consultant services, equipment, and materials your project will require and of the relationship between these elements and your objectives. It should be thought of as a tool to help you take into account *all* the costs of completing the methods and activities in your plans and document the costs that will be borne by each partner in the agreement.

If you are not familiar with spreadsheets, the Project Planner can seem a bit overwhelming. But remember, the only real mistakes you can make when completing it are mathematical (incorrect addition, multiplication, and so on). You control how detailed your Project Planner is. It should work for you.

Project Planner Example

Exhibit 10.2 on page 94 provides you with some insight into one way the Project Planner can be completed.

In this example the project director's salary is being requested from the funder, as are the salaries of two graduate students who will assist the project director. The services of the project director and the graduate students are being contracted from West State University. Therefore, their time commitments and costs fall in columns J, K, and L (Consultants/ Contract Services) on the Project Planner.

The project director, Dr. Smith, will have West State University's Human Subjects Institutional Review Board examine the procedures to get the student, parents, and teachers to agree to write contracts for change. It is anticipated that he will work on the project for twelve weeks—approximately half-time—during months one through six, and twenty-four weeks (full-time) during months seven through twelve.

The example shows a considerable amount of matching and in-kind contributions, as indicated by the asterisks. For example, the school district is donating the salary and fringe benefits for the project secretary. In addition, a significant portion of the matching and in-kind contributions is coming from the Jones Corporation, which is donating the use of its corporate video production facility.

Matching and in-kind contributions demonstrate frugality, commitment, and hard work, but "overmatching" can become an issue. When a proposal has a huge matching component and requires only a small amount of grant funds, a prospective grantor may get the impression that the entire proposal should be funded through matching and in-kind contributions. However, grantors view most matching components very favorably.

Exhibit 10.2

SAMPLE PROJECT PLANNER

PROJECT PLANNER

PROJECT TITLE: A Contract for Educational Change – Parents, Students, and Teachers Charting a Course of Responsibility

Proposal Developed for: _____ Project Director: _____ Proposed Start Date: _____ Proposed Year: _____

A. List project objectives or outcomes A. B. / B. List methods to accomplish each objective as A-1, A-2,... B-1, B-2...	Month Begin–End (C/D)	Time (E)	Project Personnel (F)	Salaries & Wages (G)	Fringe Benefits (H)	Total (I)	Time (J)	Cost/Week (K)	Total (L)	Item (M)	Cost/Item (N)	Quantity (O)	Tot cost (P)	Total I,L,P (Q)	Item (R)	Date (S)
Objective A: Increase educational cooperation of teachers, parents, and students by 25% as measured on the Responsible Educational Practices (REP) survey in 12 months at a cost of $	1/12															
A-1 Administer the survey on sample	1/3															
Project Dir (PD) & 2 graduate assistants		4w	PD	West State U			4w	1000	4000	REP Surveys	2.00	500	1000			
(Grad) administer survey, analyze,		3w	2 Grad							Mail Surveys	.50	500	250			
and input results							6w	500	3000	Phone Follow Up	1.00*	200	200*			
A-2 Develop and teach curriculum.	3/6															
a. Instruct parents, students, and teachers on responsible use of time, homework, responsibility, and contracts for change		3w / 6w	3 Trainer / PD	9000*		9000*	6w	1000	6000	Mail Invites	.50	1200	600			
b. Teach all parties how the homework responsibility system will work and how the homework hot line can be accessed and used.	3/6	3w	2 Grad				6w	500	3000	Refreshments	250		250			
A-3 Set up computer system to handle homework assignments and hot line.	1/3															
a. Purchase system hardware and software upgrades.		2w	Tech Coord	2000*	500*	2500*				Hardware / Software	8000 / 2000	1 / 1	8000 / 2000			
b. Install phone lines to handle system.		1w	Phone Co							Install Lines	2000*		2000*			
A-4 Implement the program.	6/12															
a. Set up K-12 instructional program on system.		10w	PD				10w	1000	10000	Access System	1000	6	6000			
		5w	1 Grad				5w	500	2500	for 6 Months						
A-5 Evaluate effectiveness of project.	12/12															
a. Posttest with Responsible Educational Practices survey.		2w / 1w	PD / 1 Grad				2w / 1w	1000 / 500	2000 / 500	REP Survey	2.00	500	1000			
b. Report log of usage on hot line.		2w / 1w	PD / 1 Grad				2w / 1w	1000 / 500	2000 / 500	Mail	.50	500	250			
c. Survey teachers and students on impact of grades and test scores.		2w / 1w	PD / 1 Grad				2w / 1w	1000 / 500	2000 / 500	Phone Follow	1.00*	200	200*			
Total Direct Costs or Costs Requested From Funder						0			36000				19350	55350	80%	
Matching Funds, In-Kind Contributions, or Donated Costs						11500*			0			*	2400	13900	20%	
Total Costs						11500			36000				21750	69250	100%	

©David G. Bauer Associates, Inc.
(800) 836-0732

Chapter 11

Writing Government Grant Proposals

COMPLETING A FEDERAL government proposal is very much like filing an income tax return. As with tax returns, the directions are longer than the actual forms, but the forms are not really that complicated. If you follow the Federal Grants Clock shown in Figure 7.1, make preproposal contact, and secure a copy of a funded proposal, you have an advantage over the applicant who is trying to guess what the grantor wants.

A federal grant application must be completed exactly as prescribed in the rules. The basic format and the specific order of the parts of a federal proposal are usually similar for all applications. In addition to providing an abstract or summary, the prospective grantee is normally required to identify the need, the plan to address the need, the key personnel who will operate the program, the budget, how the success of the project will be evaluated, the adequacy of resources, assurances, and attachments.

The points assigned to each area and the distribution of any additional or extra points are outlined in each agency's specific proposal guidelines. Most important, however, is that your proposal be easily understood by the reviewer. The reviewer must be able to read the proposal rapidly, and the salient parts must be evident and well documented so that a point value can be assigned to each.

Proposal Abstract

Some proposals require an abstract or summary. Often this must fit into a designated space or specific number of lines or pages. There is some controversy over when the abstract should be written. Some experts believe it should be written last, when the grant writer can reflect on the completed proposal; others contend that writing it first helps the grantee focus on preparing the proposal. Writing a detailed outline, then the proposal, and then an abstract that reviews the proposal usually works well. Whenever you write it, make sure it is in the required format. The abstract should provide a short, concise picture of need, objectives, solution, and evaluation.

In an effort to keep within the space limitations, some grant writers push the abstract to the margins and cram in as much information as possible. The result is usually difficult to read and very confusing. When you consider that the reviewer may have already read several proposals, a crammed abstract may set a negative tone for the entire proposal and lead to a low score. It may help to review the criteria that will be used to evaluate your proposal and use more of the limited space on those areas that will receive the highest priority.

Review the following abstract and consider whether it sets the stage properly. Ask yourself if it shows that the grantseeker has command of the need and that the project has measurable objectives, provides a synopsis of methods, and presents the proposal's main points in an interesting manner.

> *This project will identify those students at risk for dropping out, will intervene and provide the motivation and tools necessary to complete their high school education, and will encourage postsecondary education and training. Over a three-year period, this project will extend services to 450 students including five elementary programs that feed into three middle schools, which in turn feed into two high-school programs. Activities in this project will increase coping and daily living skills through classroom instruction, use community volunteers to tutor students and act as role models, increase awareness and incentive through two field trips, as well as track school attendance and classroom progress acting as a mediator between teachers, parents, and students to resolve problems as they arise.*

It is not a wonderful example, but this abstract does indicate that services will be extended to 450 students, five elementary programs, and three middle schools. In addition, it provides a rough idea of the types of activities aimed at keeping students in school. However, it does not even hint at the need or give any measurement indicators or criteria for success. Also, based on the abstract, the project seems geared to high schools, which makes one wonder why elementary and middle schools are even mentioned. But before we get too critical, we should note that the project summarized in this abstract was funded for approximately $97,000!

Needs Statement

This section may be referred to as the "search of relevant literature," the "extent of the need," or the "problem." One federal program refers to the needs statement as the "criterion: Extent to which the project meets specific needs recognized in the statute that authorized the program, including consideration of the needs addressed by the project; how the needs were identified; how the needs will be met; and the benefits to be gained by meeting the needs."

One successful grantee responded to this criterion with a description of the extent of the need that included the following:

1. *Target Area:* Where the applicant was located and data that identified a significant needs population in the student body

2. *Need for Services:* What school programs were available and the gap between what was and what should be

3. *How the Needs Would Be Met:* A general description of what was to be done

4. *Benefits to Be Gained:* The anticipated positive outcomes of the project

When developing the needs section, take into consideration the type of reviewer who will be reading the proposal. The needs section should be motivating and compelling. It must demonstrate that the applicant has credibility and a command of the current literature in the field. Many excellent proposals lose crucial points when the grantee fails to command the respect of the reviewer by overlooking the needs section and placing the emphasis on the project description and plan of operation.

The following "extent of the need" has been taken from a grant funded by the Department of Education for dropout prevention.[1]

The target population to be served by the project has experienced low academic achievement, high public-assistance rates, high dropout rates, linguistic and cultural differences, geographic isolation, and inaccessibility to existing career and training information. These conditions have combined to create high unemployment, underemployment, poor self-image, and a resultant low standard of living among these people.
Astin's study of college attrition clearly identifies family income as a significant factor which negatively impacts student success in post secondary education and contributes to high dropout rates. Astin does note, however, that this correlation is influenced by such other "mediation" factors as ability, motivation, financial concerns, and parental education.
. . . The target population occupies a rural mountainous and desert region covering over 8,000 square miles, which is larger than the combined area of Delaware, Rhode Island and Connecticut.

---

1. Proposal: Four Corners School, College and University Partnership Program, submitted to U.S. Department of Education, Division of Student Services, CDFA 84-204, by San Juan School District College of Eastern Utah-San Juan Campus, Utah Navajo Development Council, July 9, 1988.

. . . It is pertinent to note that 79.3 percent of the active job applicants are ethnic minority and that 63.5 percent had less than a high school diploma.[2]

Facts like those presented in this excerpt tell the reviewer and the federal staff that the writer knows how things are. Including statistics in the needs section of a proposal shows a command of the situation and can make a positive impression, unlike statements that begin "Everyone knows the need for . . . ", "Current statistics show . . . ", "It is a shame our students do not have . . . ", "You can't believe the number of times . . . ", "Several [many, an increasing number] students . . . ", and the like.

When reviewers read such weak, banal statements, they take their frustration out on the scoring sheet. A strong needs statement requires facts, studies, and references, and it takes commitment and hard work to gather these. But remember, you will be repaid in grants success!

Plan of Operation

Your government application may refer to this section as the "plan of operation," "objectives and methods," or "project methodology." The purpose of this section is to describe an organized solution to the need and problem you have identified.

Chapter Nine outlines how to construct behavioral and measurable objectives. By reviewing a previously funded proposal you can get a good idea of how the grantor prefers the plan of operation to be presented.

Review the following sample objectives. They were taken from a proposal for an early intervention dropout program. Keep in mind that the proposal was funded for $750,000!

1. *1,500 kindergarten through sixth grade at-risk students will benefit from the District's effort to institutionalize instructional improvement and variation by comprehensively upgrading all instructional and support services. This will include: attendance monitoring and immediate follow-up on absences; ombudsmen and advocates for students; junior high at-risk students tutoring of early grade at-risk students; extended school day programs; and off-site activities.*

2. *Seventy-five kindergarten through sixth grade teachers and two paraprofessionals will receive training on topics such as: implementation of effective school postulates, individualizing instruction, thematic instruction, ombudsmen and advocates for stu-*

---

2. Alexander W. Astin, *Preventing Students from Dropping Out*, San Francisco: Jossey-Bass, 1977.

dents, the city as a resource, training parents, managing at-risk student programs, and understanding the needs of ethnic minority (especially Hispanic American) and low income students.

3. *Approximately 500 parents of at-risk students will attend 30 to 60 hours of project-sponsored activities focusing on issues such as: basic literacy, parenting, how to help your child with homework, English as a second language, and social issues information about: drug and alcohol abuse, AIDS, teenage pregnancy, and suicide.*

4. *The results of this program will be publicized and disseminated. Strategies will include: a recruitment video, a video that showcases the progress and achievements of students, a program brochure, TV spot announcements, and presentations at community events.*

Do these objectives describe what will be accomplished or how the project will be done? For three-quarters of a million dollars, we should be told in what area we can expect to see change and how much.

Just because an objective contains numbers does not mean it is well constructed. This example tells us the number of parents to be trained but not what the parents will do differently as a result of the training or what impact the parental training will have on children staying in school.

The following objective is from another project funded by the Department of Education under a different program. It demonstrates the measurable component of an objective much more effectively.

By June 1, 1999, at least 65 percent of all students enrolled in the academic year program will improve at least 1.5 grade levels in mathematics, language mechanics, language expression, and reading ability as documented by pre-post Comprehensive Tests of Basic Skills scores.

Methods and Activities

Review Chapter Ten on developing a Project Planner. The Project Planner encourages an organized approach to developing your proposed plan. Whether or not you use such a planner, your proposal will be evaluated on the thoroughness and clarity of the steps prescribed. Again, a copy of a previously funded proposal gives you insight on how past grantees organized this section.

There are many ways to present objectives and methods. In the following example, the successful grantseeker first presents a main objective, then a subobjective or process objective, and finally the methodologies.

OBJECTIVE 3: UPGRADE BASIC SKILLS

PROCESS OBJECTIVE 3.1: Students will be counseled and tutored during the academic year program to meet their individual academic needs and overcome areas of deficiency.

Methodologies:

a)   *Deficiencies of participants will be documented through use of CTBS scores, transcripts, and interviews with teachers, parents, students and counselors. Through this process and individual education, a plan will be prepared based on areas of strengths, but particularly on areas of weakness in which the student needs help. This will be in the form of a contract which the student and counselor will sign to agree to work together to strengthen the academic skills which need improvement.*

b)   *The counselor will schedule bi-weekly, after-school tutoring and counseling sessions to provide academic assistance as well as emotional support.*

Personnel Responsible: Project counselors, tutors, and teachers from each high school.

Resources: Textbooks, testing and teaching materials, media centers of each high school.

Quality of Key Personnel

This section tells the reviewer how qualified your project staff is to meet the objectives and close the gap between what is and what ought to be.

One dilemma proposal developers face is that their key personnel often have not been hired by the time the proposal is submitted. If so, the proposal should clearly show that capable staff can be found. Even reviewers who have worked their way through most of a proposal want to be certain of the quality of the individuals who will implement the project.

Review the following sample taken from a funded Department of Education grant.

Criterion: The quality of the key personnel the applicant plans to use in the project. Staff will consist of a full-time project director, a full-time assistant project director, four part-time regular school year counselors, four full-time summer counselors, eight college and peer tutors, 12 part-time instructors, and a full-time secretary. Inasmuch as project staff have not been identified at this time, resumes are not included. The partnership would like to affirm that no problems are anticipated in acquiring qualified, experienced, highly competent personnel. At least one week will be scheduled at the beginning of the project for the orientation of staff to the goals, objectives, plan of operation, etc.

Do you feel confident that this applicant has the expertise necessary to conduct this project? Does the grantee's statement that "no problems are anticipated in acquiring qualified . . . personnel" make you feel comfortable? This is like betting on a horse you know nothing about simply because someone assures you it will be a winner. Every grantor wants to know the track record of people who will be working on the project.

In the example, the applicant could have stated that the project director would be reporting to Dr. Smith, who is currently responsible for managing X million dollars. However, the prospective grantee did at least follow the key personnel criterion with a detailed description of the major positions mentioned in the body of the proposal.

Note that many government grantors look for the *appropriate* use of personnel. If you are thinking about minimally involving one outstanding person in many grants, you should be aware that some funders ask for an outline of the time each staff member will commit to the project; some federal grants require that the project director or principal investor commit a certain percentage of time to the project. In other words, one outstanding and well-known individual should not commit 2 percent of his or her time to fifty projects!

Budget and Cost-Effectiveness

Federal programs' proposal requirements may differ, but all applications require a budget. In most cases, the amount of the proposal (the dollar request) is divided by the number of students who will benefit from the project so that the federal program officer can arrive at a cost per student served. One of the primary concerns of a reviewer is that the budget request be reasonable based on the steps outlined in the proposal. For example, if a project is meant to be a model for other schools, it must be affordable enough to be replicated.

The following sample is from a successful federally funded proposal. The references to cost per student have been omitted to prevent the reader from calculating a "preferred" cost figure; there is no one best equation, for the proper cost depends on the project in question.

Reasonableness of Budget

Criterion: *Costs are reasonable in relation to the objective of the project.*

Salaries and benefits are based upon institutional schedules and policies. Supplies have been computed on the basis of local vendor prices. Travel and communication costs in such a geographically isolated location may appear to be rather extensive. These have been kept to a minimum with rates on institutional policies.

The overall cost per participant from federal funds amounts to $_____ the first year, decreasing to $_____ the second year, and $_____ the third year. The budget is reasonable and cost effective, particularly considering the geographic location of the target area.

A budget narrative may also be required. A budget narrative is an explanation of how the salaries, consultant services, equipment, and materials are related to the completion of each method or activity.

The Department of Education's most common budget information form for nonconstruction projects is Standard Form (SF)-424A. If you have completed a Project Planner (see Chapter Ten), you already have all the information you need to complete the SF-424A or any other form the federal grantor may require. The preferred budget form will be included in your federal application package.

If possible, review the budget and cash forecast format of a successfully funded proposal.

Evaluation

If you developed your objectives according to the methods suggested in Chapter Nine, you have already outlined your basic steps for evaluation. Most projects demand some sort of preassessment survey so that baseline data can be gathered. After the completion of the intervention steps or the model project, the original baseline data can be compared with posttest evaluation data to demonstrate change in the target population or problem.

Using outside or external consultants to evaluate a project is looked upon by many reviewers as a positive step because this may encourage an unbiased, independent evaluation. Discuss this important section of your proposal with your prospective grantor to gather as much insight as possible into its evaluation preferences.

The evaluation section of your proposal must clearly delineate the following:

- What will be evaluated
- When the pre- and postevaluations will occur
- How much change is predicted
- Who will perform the evaluation
- How much the evaluation component will cost

In the example provided on the Sample Project Planner (see Figure 10.2), West State University was included so that the grantee did not end up evaluating its own work. By including a few West State University professors in the proposal the grantee also built credibility and demonstrated the efficient use of available local resources. Using West State University's computer resources and graduate students in the evaluation also demonstrated the cost-effectiveness of the grantee's proposal.

Adequacy of Resources

The information in this section should be included in every proposal whether or not the funding source requests it because it lets the funder know why it should make a grant to *your* school. You need to identify what makes your school a more logical choice than any other one in the area. By focusing on the problem and proposed solution, you make your school the strongest candidate for receiving the grant.

The areas that most federal grantors and reviewers are influenced by include equipment, supplies, and facilities.

- *Equipment:* Demonstrate that you have enough standard office equipment (desks, chairs, and so on) to support the additional staff called for in your proposal. If your proposal calls for nonstandard equipment such as modems and VCRs, and you are not requesting funds from the grantor to purchase these items, make it clear in your proposal that such equipment is being donated by you, the grantee, to the project. Your assurance that this equipment is available demonstrates that you have adequate resources.

- *Supplies and Materials:* Any supplies and materials that you will make available should also be noted. This will help build your case.

- *Facilities:* Describe the facilities that will be used to support the project, especially unique or different types of facilities such as computer labs, swimming pools, and so on. If your proposal involves another organization, show how its facilities and yours will be jointly used or shared to ensure the successful completion of the project.

Assurances

Your school officials will be required to provide signed assurances that the project will abide by a myriad of federal rules and regulations. Assurances deal with a wide range of issues, from drug-free workplaces to political lobbying. Your district's main office has probably signed assurances in the past and will be able to assist you in this process. For your general information, the *Catalog of Federal Domestic Assistance* outlines the required federal assurances.

One area of assurances that many school districts overlook is human subjects review. It is not necessary for your school district to organize an Institutional Review Board (IRB) to examine every federal proposal to assure that the human subjects involved are treated humanely; however, as a grantee you should develop a relationship with your local college or university so that you can arrange to have its IRB review and approve your federal proposals when appropriate.

Attachments

Reactive grantseeking limits the time available to write your proposal, often causing applications to be submitted without letters of support and agreement from cooperating organizations and community groups. This is a red flag to reviewers and often diminishes grantees' credibility and costs them valuable points. Be sure to take the time to gather your letters of support and agreement. Include them as attachments.

When possible, it is a good idea to include your Project Planner also. Other attachments may include maps, pictures, a layout of your school's building, support data for the statement of need, surveys, and questionnaires.

Reviewers find it helpful when you refer to the attachments in the body of your proposal and include a separate table of contents for the attachment section.

Chapter 12

Improving and Submitting Your Federal Grant Application

THE MAIN PURPOSE of this chapter is to provide you with a method of improving your federal proposal. The quality of your proposal influences how reviewers and agency staff members will view you and your school for many years to come. Just as teachers do not easily forget the first impression a student makes, reviewers and federal staff members do not easily forget the first impression made by a proposal.

If you and your peers review your proposal before submitting it, you will feel more confident that you are sending the prospective grantor your best effort. And even if your proposal is not selected for funding, you can be certain it was rejected because of the competition and not because of careless mistakes.

If you're like most grantseekers, by now you are tired of the whole process and what you really want to do is submit your proposal and get it out of your life. But after coming this far you shouldn't jeopardize all your hard work by submitting a proposal that hasn't passed the last test: a mock review.

The beginning of this primer explained Festinger's Theory of Cognitive Dissonance and how you must view grantseeking from the funder's perspective rather than your own. You also need to review the proposal from the funder's perspective rather than your own.

The more you know about the review system used by federal agencies, the easier it will be to perform a mock review. Through preproposal contact you should have learned how the granting agency selects reviewers, the reviewers' backgrounds, and which review system they follow. Having this information ensures that your mock review is as much like the real review as possible.

The term *quality circle* best describes the process. Invite a small group of individuals who are dedicated to improving education to participate in the circle. The participants need not be experts in the grants area or in the particular subject area of your proposal. You do want them to mirror the types of reviewers on the real federal review committee, but you should also invite several individuals with a fresh outlook to participate. For example, ask a business leader from your Grants Advisory Group, a college student, a secretary, or an accountant to be mock reviewers. These many different perspectives will give your quality circle a better chance of uncovering all or most of your proposal's weaknesses and strengths.

Either telephone individuals or ask them in person to participate. Brief them on the general approach you want them to take. It is important to begin by stating that you want to submit the best possible proposal and that a review by a quality circle will help you achieve that goal. You should also let them know that you, your close associates, and your Grants Advisory Group members are so involved in the proposal that you need a fresh perspective. Tell them you will send a package that includes a description of the types of reviewers and the evaluation or scoring system that will be used. Assure them that they do not have to be experts in the subject area but that they must make every attempt to read the proposal from the real reviewers' point of view. Use the sample letter in Exhibit 12.1 to invite individuals to participate in your quality circle.

Each federal agency that makes grants follows a different proposal review system and evaluation criteria. For instance, the National Science Foundation's system is very different from that of the National Endowment for the Humanities, and the latter is much different from the system used by the Department of Education. The fact that proposal-review systems vary in selection criteria and scoring emphasizes the need for preproposal contact with the funder and early data gathering about the review process.

The Education Department uses a review system known as Education Department General Administrative Regulations (EDGAR). Not all programs in the Education Department follow EDGAR; some have their own published regulations with a specific set of criteria. However, if the program does not have a set of published guidelines, you can assume they follow EDGAR.

EDGAR's main areas of evaluation are these:

1. How the proposed project meets the purposes of the authorizing statute

2. The extent of the need for the project

3. How the plan of operation meets the need

4. The availability of qualified key personnel to implement the plan

---

Exhibit 12.1

SAMPLE LETTER INVITING INDIVIDUAL TO PARTICIPATE IN FEDERAL PROPOSAL QUALITY CIRCLE

Date

Name
Address

Dear _____:

   I would like to take this opportunity to follow up on our conversation to secure your input in helping our school district submit the very best grant proposal possible. We are asking that you review the enclosed proposal from the point of view of a federal reviewer. The attached materials will help you role-play the actual manner in which this proposal will be evaluated.

   Please read the information on the reviewers' backgrounds and the scoring system and limit the time you spend reading the proposal to the time constraints that the real reviewers will observe. A Quality Circle Scoring Worksheet has been provided to assist you in recording your scores and comments.

   A meeting of all the mock reviewers comprising our quality circle has been scheduled for [date]. Please bring this worksheet with you to the meeting. The meeting will last less than one hour. Its purpose is to analyze the scores and brainstorm suggestions to improve the proposal.

Sincerely,
[Name]
[Phone Number]

---

5. Whether the budget is cost-effective and realistic with the respect to the plan of operation

6. How the plan's progress in meeting the objectives will be evaluated

7. Whether the applicant possesses sufficient resources to house the project and support the plan

   To help your volunteers review and evaluate your proposal from the proper perspective, you may wish to provide them with the Selection Criteria Overview and Scoring Distribution in Exhibits 12.2 and 12.3.

   Try to learn from the granting agency where and how the review occurs, the average time reviewers spend reading each proposal, and the number of proposals each reviewer is responsible for evaluating.

   At the very least, you must give your quality circle members the point system and time constraints they should abide by. Volunteer reviewers often want to do such a good job that in their zeal they spend much more time reviewing your proposal than the real reviewers will.

   Ask the volunteers to read your proposal and to designate with an asterisk those areas they think the reviewer will like and those they think will be viewed negatively. Obviously, the negative areas should be improved prior to submission.

Exhibit 12.2

SELECTION CRITERIA OVERVIEW

Meeting the Purposes of the Authorizing Statute   (5 pts)

1. What are the purposes of the authorizing statute?

2. What are the objectives of this project?

3. How will these objectives further the purposes of the authorizing statute?

Extent of Need for the Project   (25 pts)

1. What needs are outlined by the authorizing statute?

2. What needs does the applicant identify?

3. How did the applicant identify those needs? That is, what specific documentation or evidence does the application offer to support the applicant's assessment of need?

4. Are the needs identified by the applicant consistent with the purposes of the authorizing statute?

5. Does the applicant identify too many or too few needs for the proposed time frame and resources of the project?

6. Are the outlined needs well defined so that the project can be focused on them, or are they generic?

Plan of Operation   (20 pts)

1. Do the project objectives serve the purposes of the authorizing statute?

2. How well is the project designed? Are project objectives consistent with stated needs? Are project activities consistent with project objectives? Are project objectives measurable?

3. How will the applicant use its resources and personnel to achieve each objective?

4. Has the applicant developed an effective management plan that will ensure proper and efficient administration of the project?

5. Do project milestones represent a logical progression of times and tasks?

6. Does the applicant propose a realistic time schedule for accomplishing objectives?

7. Will the proposed activities accomplish the project's objectives successfully?

8. Are the planned educational approaches based on sound research that indicates they will be successful for the population to be served?

9. Does the project have clearly developed provisions for providing equal access to eligible participants who are members of traditionally underrepresented groups (racial or ethnic minorities, women, handicapped persons, elderly persons)?

Quality of Key Personnel   (15 pts)

1. Do the job descriptions adequately reflect skills needed to make the project work?

2. Are the duties of personnel clearly defined?

3. What relevant qualifications do the proposed personnel possess, especially the project director? (Focus on their experience and training in fields related to the objectives of the project, though other information may be considered.)

(continued)

Exhibit 12.2 (continued)

4. Will proposed personnel need to be trained for the project?

5. How much time will the proposed personnel actually devote to the project?

6. To what extent does the applicant encourage employment applications from members of traditionally underrepresented groups (ethnic or racial minorities, women, handicapped persons, elderly persons)?

Budget and Cost Effectiveness   (10 pts)

1. Is the budget adequate to support the project's proposed activities?

2. Are overall project costs reasonable in relation to project objectives?

3. How much of the project's total cost is devoted to administrative costs?

4. Are budget items sufficiently justified?

5. Is the budget padded?

Evaluation Plan   (15 pts)

1. Are the proposed methods of evaluation appropriate to the project?

2. Will the proposed evaluation be objective?

3. Will the proposed evaluation methods measure the effectiveness of project activities in meeting project objectives?

4. Will the evaluation plan produce valid and reliable data concerning the accomplishment of project objectives?

5. Does the evaluation plan measure the project's effect on the project audience?

Adequacy of Resources   (10 pts)

1. Are the proposed facilities adequate for project purposes?

2. Is the proposed equipment adequate for project purposes?

3. Does the applicant have access to special sources of experience or expertise?

Send or give your volunteer reviewers the Quality Circle Scoring Worksheet in Exhibit 12.4 and any other information you can gather that will assist them in their role playing. For example, information on last year's grantees may be useful, especially if the grantee mix is likely to remain the same.

You can perform the review by mail or ask the volunteers to get together for a short meeting to review the scores and discuss the proposal's positive and negative points. The members of the circle may not want to hurt your feelings by criticizing the proposal in your presence, so ask a friend to facilitate the meeting for you.

Be sure to remind your volunteer reviewers to mention your proposal's positive areas in their evaluations. In most cases, individuals tend to

Exhibit 12.3

SCORING DISTRIBUTION WORKSHEET

The numerical scores you assign to an application's response to the selection criteria must be consistent with the comments you write. Comments and scores should reflect the same overall assessment. You should never attempt to mitigate a negative comment with a positive score, or vice versa.

Comments indicate whether the application's response to the selection criteria is poor, adequate, or good; scores indicate how poor, adequate, or good. If 10 points are possible, 0–2 is poor, 3–4 is weak, 5–7 is adequate, 8–9 is superior, and 10 is outstanding. Four points means the response is merely weak, whereas 8 indicates it is above average or superior. Whatever total points are possible, use the midpoint as adequate and choose your scores accordingly. Do not hesitate to use the full range of points. It is perfectly acceptable to assign a score of 10 or 0, for example. Your guiding rule should be consistency.

Always go back and check your scores to make sure that you have written them correctly and used the appropriate point scale. You should also double-check the scores on the summary page of the Technical Review Form to make sure that they match the scores listed under each selection criterion and that the final total has been computed without error.

You may want to use the following table as a guide when assigning points:

Total	Poor	Weak	Adequate	Superior	Outstanding
25	0–8	9–12	13–19	20–23	24–25
20	0–6	7–9	10–15	16–18	19–20
15	0–4	5–7	8–11	12–13	14–15
10	0–2	3–4	5–7	8–9	10
5	0–1	2	3	4	5

focus on the negatives, although it's also important for you to know what parts of your proposal look good.

Review the scores each section of your proposal received. Based on the volunteers' scores and comments, identify the areas that need to be improved and those that should remain the same.

Submission

The Standard Form (SF) 424 (Exhibit 12.5) must be attached to the front of your federal grant application or proposal. Instructions for its completion have also been included (Exhibit 12.6). Follow the specific rules for the number of copies, front to back printing, and how to hold the proposal together.

Do not bind your proposal or staple it together unless you have checked with the federal funder. Federal funders usually prefer pressure tension clips so that forms can be added or removed as needed.

Exhibit 12.4

QUALITY CIRCLE SCORING WORKSHEET

The following information is being provided to assist you in reviewing the attached federal grant application/proposal.

The Setting—The proposals are read at:

_____ The reviewer's location

_____ The federal agency's location

_____ Another site selected by the federal agency

The Time Factor

Number of proposals the reviewer evaluates: _____

Amount of time the reviewer spends evaluating each proposal: _____

Areas to Be Scored	Points/Area	Comments/Suggestions

Total Points for Proposal

_____

What is the background and training of the evaluators? _____

_____

_____

What point system will be followed? _____

_____

_____

How much time will be spent reviewing each proposal? _____

_____

Use this space to note anything special that will affect proposal outcome. _____

_____

_____

_____

_____

_____

Exhibit 12.5

STANDARD FORM (SF) 424

OMB Approval No. 0348-004

APPLICATION FOR FEDERAL ASSISTANCE	2. DATE SUBMITTED	Applicant Identifier

1. TYPE OF SUBMISSION	3. DATE RECEIVED BY STATE	State Application Identifier

Application Preapplication

☐ Construction ☐ Construction

☐ Non-Construction ☐ Non-Construction	4. DATE RECEIVED BY FEDERAL AGENCY	Federal Identifier

5. APPLICANT INFORMATION

Legal Name: Organizational Unit:

Address (give city, county, state and zip code):   Name and telephone number of the person to be contacted on matters involving this application (give area code):

6. EMPLOYER IDENTIFICATION NUMBER (EIN):

☐☐ ☐☐☐☐☐☐☐

7. TYPE OF APPLICANT: (enter appropriate letter in box) ☐

A. State   H. Independent School District
B. County   I. State Controlled Institution of Higher Learning
C. Municipal   J. Private University
D. Township   K. Indian Tribe
E. Interstate   L. Individual
F. Intermunicipal   M. Profit Organization
G. Special District   N. Other (Specify):

8. TYPE OF APPLICATION

☐ New   ☐ Continuation   ☐ Revision

If Revision, enter appropriate letter(s) in box(es): ☐ ☐
A. Increase Award   B. Decrease Award   C. Increase Duration
D. Decrease Duration   Other (specify): _____

9. NAME OF FEDERAL AGENCY

10. CATALOG OF FEDERAL DOMESTIC ASSISTANCE NUMBER   [8][4][ ][ ][ ]
    TITLE:

11. DESCRIPTIVE TITLE OF APPLICANT'S PROJECT:

12. AREA AFFECTED BY PROJECT (cities, counties, states, etc.):

13. PROPOSED PROJECT:		14. CONGRESSIONAL DISTRICTS OF:	
Start Date	Ending Date	a. Applicant	b. Project

15. ESTIMATED FUNDING:

a. Federal	$	.00
b. Applicant	$	.00
c. State	$	.00
d. Local	$	.00
e. Other	$	.00
f. Program Income	$	.00
g. Total	$	.00

16. IS APPLICATION SUBJECT TO REVIEW BY STATE EXECUTIVE ORDER 12372 PROCESS?

a. YES   THIS PREAPPLICATION/APPLICATION WAS MADE AVAILABLE TO THE STATE EXECUTIVE ORDER 12372 PROCESS FOR REVIEW ON:

DATE: _____

b. NO   ☐ PROGRAM IS NOT COVERED BY E.O. 12372

☐ OR PROGRAM HAS NOT BEEN SELECTED BY STATE FOR REVIEW

17. IS THE APPLICANT DELINQUENT ON ANY FEDERAL DEBT?

☐ Yes If "Yes" attach an explanation   ☐ No

18. TO THE BEST OF MY KNOWLEDGE AND BELIEF, ALL DATA IN THIS APPLICATION / PREAPPLICATION ARE TRUE AND CORRECT. THE DOCUMENT HAS BEEN DULY AUTHORIZED BY THE GOVERNING BODY OF THE APPLICANT AND THE APPLICANT WILL COMPLY WITH THE ATTACHED ASSURANCES IF THE ASSISTANCE IS AWARDED.

a. Typed Name of Authorized Representative	b. Title	c. Telephone Number
d. Signature of Authorized Representative		e. Date Signed

Previous Editions Not Usable   Standard Form 424 (Rev 4-88)

Authorized for Local Reproduction   Prescribed by OMB Circular A-102

Exhibit 12.6

INSTRUCTIONS FOR THE SF 424

This is a standard form used by applicants as a required facesheet for preapplications and applications submitted for Federal assistance. It will be used by Federal agencies to obtain applicant certification that States which have established a review and comment procedure in response to Executive Order 12372 and have selected the program to be included in their process, have been given an opportunity to review the applicant's submission.

1. Self-explanatory.

2. Date application submitted to Federal agency (or State if applicable) & applicant's control number (if applicable).

3. State use only (if applicable).

4. If this application is to continue or revise an existing award, enter present Federal identifier number. If for a new project, leave blank.

5. Legal name of applicant, name of primary organizational unit which will undertake the assistance activity, complete address of the applicant, and name and telephone number of the person to contact on matters related to this application.

6. Enter Employer Identification Number (EIN) as assigned by the Internal Revenue Service.

7. Enter the appropriate letter in the space provided.

8. Check appropriate box and enter appropriate letter(s) in the space(s) provided:

   —"New" means a new assistance award.

   —"Continuation" means an extension for an additional funding/budget period for a project with a projected completion date.

   —"Revision" means any change in the Federal Government's financial obligation or contingent liability from an existing obligation.

9. Name of Federal agency from which assistance is being requested with this application.

10. Use the Catalog of Federal Domestic Assistance number and title of the program under which assistance is requested.

11. Enter a brief descriptive title of the project. If more than one program is involved, you should append an explanation on a separate sheet. If appropriate (e.g., construction or real property projects), attach a map showing project location. For preapplications, use a separate sheet to provide a summary description of this project.

12. List only the largest political entities affected (e.g., State, counties, cities).

13. Self-explanatory.

14. List the applicant's Congressional District and any District(s) affected by the program or project.

15. Amount requested or to be contributed during the first funding/budget period by each contributor. Value of in-kind contributions should be included on appropriate lines as applicable. If the action will result in a dollar change to an existing award, indicate *only* the amount of the change. For decreases, enclose the amounts in parentheses. If both basic and supplemental amounts are included, show breakdown on an attached sheet. For multiple program funding, use totals and show breakdown using same categories as item 15.

16. Applicants should contact the State Single Point of Contact (SPOC) for Federal Executive Order 12372 to determine whether the application is subject to the State intergovernmental review process.

17. This question applies to the applicant organization, not the person who signs as the authorized representative. Categories of debt include delinquent audit disallowances, loans and taxes.

18. To be signed by the authorized representative of the applicant. A copy of the governing body's authorization for you to sign this application as official representative must be on file in the applicant's office. (Certain Federal agencies may require that this authorization be submitted as part of the application.)

Application Transmittal

Your federal application package contains specific directions on how to transmit your proposal to Washington, D.C.

The instructions in Exhibit 12.7 are taken from the Department of Education's federal guidelines. Note that granting agencies have different rules regarding transmittal. Always check to be sure you are following the correct process. Electronic transmittal is becoming more common and as more programs try it, it will eventually become a standard. To be sure that you know what your proposal will look like when transmitted electronically, perform an internal test first. Print it out to make sure the layout, font, and overall appearance is acceptable.

The main purpose of the proactive grants system is to be able to submit your proposal early, not just on time. If you submit your proposal early, the federal bureaucrats may think that you will also submit your reports early once you are funded. This is all to the good!

Signature

Your federal grant application cover letter and assurances must be signed by an authorized district representative. Your district grants office may help you procure the necessary signatures.

Intergovernmental Review of Federal Programs

The purpose of an intergovernmental review is to provide a mechanism for coordinating funds and projects and to reduce the chances of the federal government supporting a program that the state has decided is not part of its plan. Not all programs require an intergovernmental review, and not all states have the same reporting requirements. However, if an intergovernmental review is required and your district has a grants office or a formal grants procedure, it will most likely handle the review.

If you must handle the review, contact your state's single point of contact to ensure that you comply with your state's requirements for coordinating your grant with other programs in your state. A list of State Single Points of Contact has been included for your convenience (Exhibit 12.8, pages 116–118).

Exhibit 12.7

APPLICATION TRANSMITTAL INSTRUCTIONS

An application for an award must be mailed or hand delivered by the closing date.

Applications Delivered by Mail

An application sent by mail must be addressed to the U.S. Department of Education, Application Control Center, Attention: CFDA Number _____, 400 Maryland Avenue SW, Washington, D.C. 20202-4725. An application must show proof of mailing consisting of one of the following:

- A legibly dated U.S. Postal Service postmark.
- A legible mail receipt with the date of mailing stamped by the U.S. Postal Service.
- A dated shipping label, invoice, or receipt from a commercial carrier.
- Any other proof of mailing acceptable to the U.S. Secretary of Education.

If an application is sent through the U.S. Postal Service, the Secretary does not accept either of the following as proof of mailing:

- A private metered postmark, or
- A mail receipt that is not dated by the U.S. Postal Service.

An applicant should note that the U.S. Postal Service does not uniformly provide a dated postmark. Before relying on this method, an applicant should check with the local post office.

An applicant is encouraged to use registered or at least first class mail.

Late applicants will be notified that their applications will not be considered.

Applications Delivered by Hand/Courier Service

An application that is hand delivered must be taken to the U.S. Department of Education, Application Control Center, Room 3633, General Services Administration National Capital Region, 7th and D Streets SW., Washington, D.C. 20202-4725.

The Application Control Center will accept deliveries between 8:00 a.m. and 4:30 P.M. (Washington, D.C.) daily, except Saturdays, Sundays, and federal holidays.

Individuals delivering applications must use the D Street entrance. Proper identification is necessary to enter the building.

In order for an application sent through a courier service to be considered timely, the courier service must be in receipt of the application on or before the closing date.

Exhibit 12.8

EXECUTIVE ORDER-INTERGOVERNMENTAL REVIEW

The Education Department General Administrative Regulations (EDGAR), 34 CFR 79, pertaining to intergovernmental review of Federal programs, apply to the program included in this application package.

Immediately upon receipt of this notice, all applicants, other than federally recognized Indian Tribal Governments, must contact the appropriate State Point of Contact to find out about, and to comply with the State's process under Executive Order 12372. Applicants proposing to perform in more than one State should contact, immediately upon receipt of this notice, the Single Points of Contact for each State and follow the procedures established in those States under the Executive Order. A list containing the Single Point of Contact for each State is included in the application package for this program.

In States that have not established a process or chosen a program for review, State, area wide, regional, and local entities may submit comments directly to the Department.

Any State Process Recommendation and other comments by a State Point of Contact and any comments from State, area wide, regional, and local entities must be mailed or hand-delivered by the date in the Program announcement for Intergovernmental Review to the following address:

> The Secretary
> E.O. 12372-CFDA # 84.200
> U.S. Department of Education, FB-10, Room 6213
> 600 Independence Avenue, SW
> Washington, DC 20202

In those States that require review for this program, applications are to be submitted simultaneously to the State Review Process and the U.S. Department of Education.

Proof of mailing will be determined on the same basis as applications.

Please note that the above address is not the same address as the one to which the applicant submits its completed application.

DO NOT SEND APPLICATIONS TO THE ABOVE ADDRESS.

State Single Points of Contact

In accordance with Executive Order #12372, "Intergovernmental Review Process," this listing represents the designated State Single Points of Contact. Upon request, a background document explaining the Executive Order is available. The Office of Management and Budget point of contact for updating this listing is: Donna Rivelli (202) 395-5090. The States not listed no longer participate in the process. These include: Alabama; Alaska; Kansas; Hawaii; Idaho; Louisiana; Minnesota; Montana; Nebraska; Oklahoma; Oregon; Pennsylvania; Virginia; and Washington. This list is based on the most current information provided by the States. Information on any changes or apparent errors should be provided to the Office of Management and Budget and the State in question. Changes to the list will be made only upon formal notification by the State.

ARIZONA
Ms. Janice Dunn
Arizona State Clearinghouse
3800 North Central Venue
Fourteenth Floor
Phoenix, Arizona 85012
Telephone: (602) 280-1315

ARKANSAS
Ms. Tracie L. Copeland
Manager, State Clearinghouse
Office of Intergovernmental Service
Department of Finance
  and Administration
P.O. Box 3278
Little Rock, Arkansas 72203
Telephone: (501) 371-1074

CALIFORNIA
Mr. Glenn Staber
Grants Coordinator
Office of Planning & Research
1400 Tenth Street
Sacramento, California 95814
Telephone: (916) 323-7480

(continued)

Exhibit 12.8 (continued)

COLORADO
State Single Point of Contact
State Clearinghouse
Division of Local Government
1313 Sherman Street, Room 520
Denver, Colorado 80203
Telephone: (303) 866-2156

CONNECTICUT
Mr. William T. Quigg
Intergovernmental Review
    Coordinator
State Single Point of Contact
Office of Policy and Management
Intergovernmental Policy Division
80 Washington Street
Hartford, Connecticut 06106-4459
Telephone: (203) 566-3410

DELAWARE
Ms. Francine Booth
State Single Point of Contact
Executive Department
Thomas Collins Building
Dover, Delaware 19903
Telephone: (302) 736-3326

DISTRICT OF COLUMBIA
Mr. Rodney T. Hallman
State Single Point of Contact
Office of Grants Management &
    Development
717 14th St. N.W., Suite 500
Washington, DC 20005
Telephone: (202) 727-6551

FLORIDA
Florida State Clearinghouse
Intergovernmental Affairs Policy
    Unit
Executive Office of the Governor
Office of Planning & Budgeting
The Capitol
Tallahassee, Florida 32399-0001
Telephone: (904) 488-8114

GEORGIA
Charles H. Badger, Administrator
Georgia State Clearinghouse
270 Washington Street, S.W.
Room 534A
Atlanta, Georgia 30334
Telephone: (404) 656-3855

ILLINOIS
Mr. Steve Klokkenga
State Single Point of Contact
Office of the Governor
State of Illinois
107 Stratton Building
Springfield, Illinois 62706
Telephone: (217) 782-1671

INDIANA
Ms. Jean S. Blackwell
Budget Director
State Budget Agency
212 State House
Indianapolis, Indiana 46204
Telephone: (317) 232-5610

IOWA
Mr. Steven R. McCann
Division for Community Progress
Iowa Department of Economic
    Development
200 East Grand Avenue
Des Moines, Iowa 50309
Telephone: (515) 281-3725

KENTUCKY
Mr. Ronald W. Cook
Office of the Governor
Department of Local Government
1024 Capitol Center Drive
Frankfort, Kentucky 40601
Telephone: (502) 564-2382

MAINE
State Single Point of Contact
Attn: Joyce Benson
State Planning Office
State House Station #38
Augusta, Maine 04333
Telephone: (207) 289-3261

MARYLAND
Mary Abrams, Chief
Maryland State Clearinghouse
Department of State Planning
301 West Preston Street
Baltimore, Maryland 21201
Telephone: (301) 225-4490

MASSACHUSETTS
Ms. Karen Arone
State Clearinghouse
Executive Office of Communities
    and Development
100 Cambridge Street, Room 1803
Boston, Massachusetts 02202
Telephone: (617) 727-7001

MICHIGAN
Richard S. Pastula
Director
Michigan Department of Commerce
Office of Federal Grants
P.O. Box 30225
Lansing, Michigan 48909
Telephone: (517) 373-7356

MISSISSIPPI
Ms. Cathy Mallette
Clearinghouse Officer
Office of Federal Grant Management
    and Reporting
Dept. of Finance and Administration
301 West Pearl Street
Jackson, Mississippi 39203
Telephone: (601) 949-2174

MISSOURI
Ms. Lois Pohl
Federal Assistance Clearinghouse
Office of Administration
P.O. Box 809
Room 430, Truman Building
Jefferson City, Missouri 65102
Telephone: (314) 751-4834

NEVADA
Department of Administration
State Clearinghouse
Capitol Complex
Carson City, Nevada 89710
Attn: Ron Sparks
Clearinghouse Coordinator
Telephone: (702) 687-4065

NEW HAMPSHIRE
Mr. Jeffrey H. Taylor, Director
New Hampshire Office of State
    Planning
Attn: Intergovernmental Review
    Process/James E. Bieber
2 1/2 Beacon Street
Concord, New Hampshire 03301
Telephone: (603) 271-2155

NEW JERSEY
Gregory W. Adkins, Acting Director
Division of Community Resources
NJ Dept. of Community Affairs
Direct correspondence to:
Andrew Jaskolka
State Review Process
Division of Community Resources
CN 814, Room 609
Trenton, New Jersey 08625-0814
Telephone: (609) 292-9025

(continued)

Exhibit 12.8 (continued)

NEW MEXICO
Mr. George Elliott
Deputy Director
State Budget Division
Rm 190, Bataan Memorial Building
Santa Fe, New Mexico 87503
Telephone: (505) 827-3640

NEW YORK
New York State Clearinghouse
Division of the Budget
State Capitol
Albany, New York 12224
Telephone: (518) 474-1605

NORTH CAROLINA
Mrs. Chrys Baggett, Director
Office of the Secretary of Admin.
N.C. State Clearinghouse
116 West Jones Street
Raleigh, N. Carolina 27603-8003
Telephone: (919) 733-7232

NORTH DAKOTA
North Dakota State Single Point of
     Contact
Office of Intergovernmental
     Assistance
Office of Management & Budget
600 East Boulevard Avenue
Bismarck, N. Dakota 58505-0170
Telephone: (701) 224-2094

OHIO
Mr. Larry Weaver
State Single Point of Contact
State/Federal Funds Coordinator
State Clearinghouse
Office of Budget & Management
30 East Broad Street, 34th Floor
Columbus, Ohio 43266-0411
Telephone: (614) 466-0698

RHODE ISLAND
Mr. Daniel W. Varin
Associate Director
Statewide Planning Program
Department of Administration
Division of Planning
265 Melrose Street
Providence, Rhode Island 02907
Telephone: (401) 277-2656
Please direct correspondence and
     questions to:
Review Coordinator
Office of Strategic Planning

SOUTH CAROLINA
Ms. Omeagia Burgess
State Single Point of Contact
Grant Services
Office of the Governor, Room 477
1205 Pendleton Street
Columbia, South Carolina 29201
Telephone: (803) 734-0493

SOUTH DAKOTA
Ms. Susan Comer
State Clearinghouse Coordinator
Office of the Governor
500 East Capitol
Pierre, South Dakota 57501
Telephone: (605) 733-3212

TENNESSEE
Mr. Charles Brown
State Single Point of Contact
State Planning Office
500 Charlotte Avenue
309 John Sevier Building
Nashville, Tennessee 37219
Telephone: (615) 741-1676

TEXAS
Mr. Tom Adams
Governor's Office of Budget and
     Planning
P.O. Box 12428
Austin, Texas 78711
Telephone: (512) 463-1778

UTAH
Utah State Clearinghouse
Office of Planning and Budget
Attn: Ms. Carolyn Wright
Room 116, State Capitol
Salt Lake City, Utah 84114
Telephone: (801) 538-1535

VERMONT
Mr. Bernard D. Johnson
Assistant Director
Office of Policy Research & Coord.
Pavilion Office Building
109 State Street
Montpelier, Vermont 05602
Telephone: (802) 828-3326

WEST VIRGINIA
Mr. Fred Cutlip
Director
Community Development Division
West Virginia Development Office
Building #6, Room 553
Charleston, West Virginia 25305
Telephone: (304) 348-4010

WISCONSIN
Mr. William C. Carey, Section Chief
Federal/State Relations Office
Wisconsin Department of
     Administration
101 South Webster Street
P.O. Box 7864
Madison, Wisconsin 53707
Telephone: (608) 266-0267

WYOMING
Ms. Sheryl Jeffries
State Single Point of Contact
Herschler Building
4th Floor, East Wing
Cheyenne, Wyoming 82002
Telephone: (307) 777-7574

TERRITORIES

GUAM
Mr. Michael J. Reidy, Director
Bureau of Budget and Management
     Research
Office of the Governor
P.O. Box 2950
Agana, Guam 96910
Telephone: (671) 472-2285

NORTHERN MARIANA ISLANDS
State Single Point of Contact
Planning and Budget Office
Office of the Governor
Saipan, CM
Northern Mariana Islands 96950

PUERTO RICO
Norma Burgos/Jose E. Caro
Chairman/Director
Puerto Rico Planning Board
Minillas Government Center
P.O. Box 41119
San Juan, Puerto Rico 00940-9985
Telephone: (809) 727-4444

VIRGIN ISLANDS
Mr. Jose George, Director
Office of Management & Budget
#41 Norregade Emancipation
     Garden Station, 2nd Floor
St. Thomas, Virgin Islands 00802
Please direct correspondence to:
Linda Clarke
Telephone: (809) 774-0750

Chapter 13

Writing Foundation and Corporate Proposals

PRIVATE GRANTING SOURCES use a variety of terms to refer to the format in which proposals must be submitted. Foundations and corporations may ask that you request a grant by writing a letter of inquiry, a letter proposal, a concept paper, or a preproposal letter.

But however private grantors refer to it, you must develop a distinctly different proposal for each foundation and corporation. Few private funders have application requirements that rival the federal government's, but it is imperative that you follow any instructions you do receive. For example, limitations on number of pages and attachments must be observed.

The foundation and corporate grants marketplace is very different from the federal grants arena. Private grantors have few office workers, staff, and paid reviewers and seldom have a predetermined scoring system for proposal evaluation. Some larger foundation and corporate granting programs have a specified proposal format and hire experts in the field to review proposals, but they are relatively rare. In general, proposals submitted to foundations and corporations are read by board members or trustees who have a limited amount of time to spend reviewing hundreds of proposals. Many are not experts in the areas funded by the organization, and none are professional reviewers. They are decision makers. They know what their foundation or corporation is looking for, and they answer only to their fellow trustees or board members. They prefer short proposals that can be read rapidly. This means that your proposal must stimulate their interest right from the beginning and be able to sustain it. The best way to show respect for the reader's time is to demonstrate that you have purposefully selected his or her organization and have constructed a tailored approach based on its needs.

The biggest mistake you can make in pursuing grants from foundations and corporations is to use the shotgun approach—one proposal fits all. The reader can see at a glance that the same proposal has been shotgunned to a list of prospective funders. This tells the funding source that it was lumped together with others and that its individual values and needs were ignored for the convenience of the grant writer. The forethought and effort you have invested thus far in studying the proactive grants process will keep you from shotgunning your proposals. Instead, you will use a telescopic lens to zero in on your funder. Remember, you are striving for a 50 percent or better success rate. Your foundation or corporate proposal is not a direct-mail fund-raising piece that you expect less than a 1 percent return on. The grantors you solicit represent one of the most prestigious groups of potential supporters for your school. You must present them with your best effort, not the most convenient or easiest.

The Letter Proposal

The most common type of a proposal to a foundation or corporation is written as a letter and submitted on the applicant's stationery or letterhead. Most private funders limit letter proposals to two or three pages and do not allow attachments. Even when the funder provides proposal guidelines, be sure to include the following areas in your proposal in a format the funder will find acceptable:

1. Introductory paragraph stating your reason for writing
2. Paragraph describing why you selected this particular grantor
3. Needs paragraph
4. Solution paragraph
5. Request for funds paragraph
6. Uniqueness paragraph indicating why your school should receive the grant instead of another
7. Closing paragraph
8. Signatures
9. Attachments (if allowed)

Write a draft proposal by following this outline. As you write, try to stick to the outline, writing each component in the order suggested; then edit and rearrange if necessary. Remember, the arrangement of the components should be geared to the grantor's point of view. Your proposal should follow an order that will sustain the funder's interest. Although it will be difficult, try to look at your letter proposal from the perspective of a teacher who does not know everything you know about your proposed project.

Introduction

In this section refer to any linkages or friends who have already talked to the foundation or corporate board members or trustees on your behalf. Avoid focusing on yourself. Do not begin by stating, "We are writing to you because we need . . . " The funding source knows you are writing, and what you need is not its primary concern. What it values and needs is its focus. Therefore, place the emphasis on them. For example: "John Smith suggested that I contact the Jones Foundation with an exciting project that deals with _____, an area about which our school and your board share a deep concern." It is particularly helpful with corporate grantors to mention their employees who have donated time to your school, and especially to your project. If these volunteers suggested you apply, place that information here.

Why You Selected the Grantor

Demonstrate that you have done your homework by showing off your knowledge. For foundations, analyze your research. For example, by closely examining a foundation's IRS tax return you may be able to develop an interesting fact or statistic that is not obvious and does not appear in a foundation resource publication. You could also cite an outstanding grant recipient or program previously funded by the foundation to show your familiarity with its granting pattern and history. For instance, if a foundation's tax return indicates that approximately 25 percent of its grants are related to children, you could add two years together and say something like this:

> My research indicates that in a recent two-year period, the Smith
> Foundation made _____ grants totaling over _____
> dollars for projects focusing on children and their ability to compete.
> Your granting pattern has prompted us to submit to you this proposal
> for improving our faculty's ability to involve parents in the education of
> their children attending Neighborville Middle School.

Corporate grants information is more difficult to collect and analyze than that of foundations because corporations do not have to make their records available to the public. For corporate grantors it may be necessary to gather insights through linkages, preproposal contact, or company workers who have volunteered to help you. For instance: "Harry Higgs, chairperson of our volunteer group and your employee, has stated that the Jones Corporation places a high value on quality education for young people."

In general, this section of your letter proposal should make the funder realize that you did your homework and that you believe it is special and unique. It should make the reader want to keep reading.

Although the request for funds usually appears later in the letter proposal, you can put it in this section if you choose to. This avoids the problem of having a grantor get very interested in your project only to find that the amount you ultimately request is not realistic. If you decide to put your grant request here, introduce its anticipated size by comparing your grant amount to the foundation's or corporation's average grant size for that subject area. For example: "Our research has shown that your average grant size for (subject area) is $26,500. It is with this knowledge that we encourage you to consider this grant for $25,000."

The Need for Your Project

Do not describe your project in this section. Unfortunately, overzealous grantseekers have a tendency to jump right into a description of what they want to do. You should describe your project and solution only after the funding source understands the need for any project or solution.

Review your research on the funding source. Remember, you are trying to demonstrate that there is a gap between what is and what ought to be. The more you know about the funder's values and perspective, the better you can select the appropriate documentation of need. The needs section must do the following:

- Be motivating and compelling enough to sustain the funder's interest

- Demonstrate that you have a command of the literature and the state of the art concerning the problem

- Appeal to the perspective and interests of the private grantor

Review the grants pattern of the funder. Knowing the types of projects it has funded in the past and where the projects were implemented gives you valuable insight and allows you to select and tailor the data you present in the needs section. Federal and state grantors and reviewers expect statistics, research references, and quotations, but foundation and corporate readers may be more motivated by an example, a story, or a case study. For instance, the needs section of a letter proposal to a foundation may include something like the following.

National studies have demonstrated that children watch television an average of _____ hours per day. A survey of the fourth graders at ABC Elementary School showed that their television viewing surpassed the national average by 20%. One possible reason for this disparity could be that the children from ABC Elementary School spend more time alone than many children. One fourth grader surveyed said, "I ride a bus for one hour to get home after school. I'm lonely and tired and my mom doesn't get home until late, so TV is my friend—and a lot better friend than my brother! People who say TV is violent have never lived with my brother."

It is important to determine what type of needs documentation the prospective grantor finds the most motivating. Does the funding source's distribution of past grants show any specific geographic preferences? What types of grantees have been supported in the past? Can this information help you select the right data, studies, or examples to document the need?

In respect to corporate funders, review what you know about them. Where do they have company plants or centers of operation? How can the problem addressed in your proposal affect their marketplace and products? Because corporations need well-educated workers, you will find that they are normally concerned with the educational achievement of their employees and their employees' children.

You are tailoring the needs section to the particular grantor, but you have not suggested a solution yet. The thought now should be what can be done to change the situation. We have a solution, right?

Solution

This is where you describe what can be done to solve the problem. It is often difficult to construct this section of the letter proposal in the limited space available. The previous paragraphs of the letter proposal focus on the grantor, and normally knowledge of the funding source is limited. But now it is time to describe your project—to summarize your solution—and you naturally have much more information than you can fit in a few short paragraphs. The challenge is to decide what to exclude. You must not describe your solution in such great detail that you confuse the funding source and prevent it from understanding the overall concept. This could cause you to lose funding altogether. Remember, you can always supply more information on request. The object of this section is to provide the prospective grantor with a basic understanding of the solution. To do so, ask yourself what you would want to see in the solution if you were the grantor.

The Project Planner may make it easier to keep your project summary short. If you have developed a Project Planner (see Chapter Ten) you may want to attach it to your proposal or include it within the proposal. (In the former case, be sure attachments are allowed. If not, you could make your Project Planner page two of a three-page letter proposal.) The Project Planner is a useful inclusion because it clearly shows the relationship between activities or methods and the accomplishment of the objectives. The Project Planner also provides an excellent basis for the budget section that follows, particularly when you consider that it can summarize five or more pages of narrative on one spreadsheet!

Whether or not you use a Project Planner with your letter proposal, your solution must be interesting, plausible, affordable, and well organized. The objectives should be summarized in such a manner that the funder can almost see the gap shrink between what is and what ought to be.

Your letter proposal should focus on one solution—the one with the greatest chance of matching the values of the prospective grantor. If you have done your homework, you know what it values and have described a need that will motivate agreement that the area you are addressing is important. By this point the prospective grantor should believe that the gap must be closed, and closed now. If this is the case, the funding source will not be able to put your proposal down without reading your suggested solution.

It is, however, possible for funders to disagree with your solution. Even if you did your homework, they may have values, feelings, or prejudices you did not know about. They could say that they don't think your solution will work, that they have already funded a grant that tried the same solution, or that there are other applicants with better or more interesting solutions. But if you are fortunate enough to still have their attention and they are interested in the potential benefits of the solution, the next item to be addressed in your letter proposal is cost.

Request for Funds

Grantors have limited money and receive many more proposals than they can fund. Estimates are that private funders grant only 10 percent of the requests they receive. Ultimately they must judge which projects produce what benefits for how many of the target population. The decision will ultimately be based on which grantee offers the most compelling benefits for the population the funder values.

State the amount you want. If appropriate, divide the cost of the project by the number of students the project will serve. This will give you the cost per student served. Remember that your project has a "roll-out" or future benefit because each student served will go through life with more skills, better job opportunities, and so on. If your proposal deals with parent or teacher training, roll out your project's benefits to the number of individuals these trained people will come in contact with. When dealing with facilities and equipment, identify how many will use the resource over its lifetime. For example, "X number of families will use the Middlesex Recreational Facility for Y hours over ten years." In an example like this, the cost per person served could be as little as pennies per hour!

Multiple Funders

Obviously your letter proposal must state the amount you are requesting from the grantor. However, if your project requires funding from more than one source, you should also state that you are seeking additional funds from other corporations or foundations. Avoid saying, however, that you hope to get funded by (for example) the Smith Corporation, the Jones Foundation, and so on. State the exact number of other funders being approached. Also cite grantors that have already agreed to partially fund your project. Present the total amount already received and the amount outstanding.

For jointly funded projects it is crucial that the grantors know that you are tailoring your proposal to each prospective funding source and that you have done your grants homework. Some grantors may be justifiably concerned that their part of your project will get lost in the shuffle or that they will not receive appropriate credit. To alleviate these concerns, use a colored highlighter to visually separate each grantor's part of the total project on your Project Planner and refer to it so the grantor can see how integral its portion is to the whole plan.

Matching Costs and In-Kind Contributions

Some grantors require that a portion of the project costs be borne by the grantee. Many federal grantors require matching contributions, and several foundations and corporations also require grantees to pay for part of their projects. Even if a matching or in-kind contribution is not required, you may still want to include one to demonstrate your dedication to your goal. Private grantors are concerned that the organizations they fund be committed to supporting their projects after grant funds are depleted. By demonstrating your school's commitment in advance through a matching or in-kind contribution, you show that you have not applied for the grantor's money without carefully analyzing your own commitment. Designate matching and in-kind contributions on your Project Planner with an asterisk.

If the Grantor Requests a Budget

Forty-four thousand of the forty-five thousand foundations probably do not require that you submit a budget with your letter proposal. Of the thousand or so that do, only a few hundred request that a specific budget format be used.

If you have developed a Project Planner, preparing the budget is a simple task. For a letter proposal budget, you probably just have to provide a summary of the major line items on your Project Planner. However, be sure to let the grantor know that more detailed budget information is available upon request.

If no budget format is specified, present the budget in a paragraph or block form. Use minimum space and short columns instead of long ones. Here is an example:

We are requesting a grant of $20,000 from the Smith Foundation. To demonstrate our school's support of this important project we will provide $8,000 in matching support. A detailed budget is available upon request.

	Request	Match	Total
Salaries & Wages	$10,000		$10,000
Stipends/Teachers In-Service		7,000	7,000
Consultants/Evaluation	3,000		3,000
Computer Equipment/Software	7,000		7,000
Internet Access		1,000	1,000
TOTAL	$20,000	$8,000	$28,000

Uniqueness

This section explains why your school should get the grant instead of another one. Funding sources will be asking themselves this question anyway, so why not bring it up yourself? Why *should* your school, classroom, or consortium get this grant? Couldn't another school initiate the methods and do the project just as well? The answer to the last question is no, for the following reasons.

- You developed the idea for the project! It is your baby.

- You have documented your school or classroom's need. The opportunity to act is where you are.

- You developed the idea with the help of experts in curriculum development, evaluation, and so forth. You arranged for their input, gathered them together, and worked with them. In other words, you have already invested many, many hours developing a project that will be a successful model.

Brainstorm what positive forces are at work that can convince the grantor that your school is indeed the best school to fund. For instance, in addition to superior facilities, you may also have unique individuals whose commitment and expertise make your school the funding source's most logical choice. If you are to be the project director, put in a plug for yourself. For example, "Ms. Jane Doe is slated to direct the project. Ms. Doe has been recognized as an outstanding educator by the South Dakota Department of Education and has more than 12 years of experience in classroom teaching." You can say something good about yourself because you are not going to sign the letter. Yes, that's right. Although you may write many letter proposals, you will seldom sign them. In general, they should be signed by the highest-ranking individual in your school system. So put in something complimentary about yourself. Then, when your top-ranking administrator signs it, it will become the truth!

Closing Paragraph

Use the closing paragraph to reaffirm your school's commitment to the project and to invite the funder to work with you on achieving the project's anticipated results. You should also reaffirm your willingness to provide the funding source with any additional materials that may help it make a decision. You could invite the grantor to visit your school or classroom to observe the needs firsthand.

Always include the name and phone number of your contact person in the closing paragraph. In many cases the individual whose signature appears on the proposal knows very little about the details of the project. You might say something like, "Please contact Jane Doe, the project director, at 716-358-4501 for proposal details or with any questions you may have."

Signatures

Taking the grantor's point of view into consideration, ask yourself whose signature will have the greatest impact on the funding decision. In your case, it is most likely to be the signature of your superintendent or building principal, although some schools prefer to have proposals signed by the assistant superintendent for instruction, the business officer, or the curriculum specialist. Some proposals are submitted with two signatures—the president of the school board's and a top-ranking school administrator's. It may be appropriate to have several signatures on proposals that require special cooperation, collaboration, or coordination. For example, a consortium proposal may have the signatures of all the cooperating parties.

Attachments

Most foundations and corporations do not allow or encourage attachments. Attachments may help answer questions that arise when a proposal is being read, but the problems they create for understaffed foundations and corporations often prohibit their inclusion.

What about pictures, videotapes, audiotapes, and slides? It certainly seems that in the age of electronics, these components would be allowed. However, even when you are dealing with manufacturers of electronic equipment, find out what is allowed before submitting your proposal. Although electronic tools may be highly effective in preproposal contact, they may be useless during the actual proposal review. For example, what good would it be to submit a CD or videotape with your proposal if the reviewer does not have access to playback equipment?

What's in Store for the Future?

Foundations in some states are joining together to support a standard format for grant applications. However, it is not likely that this effort will result in a standard format in the near future. If you follow the information and application guidelines in the various resource books, make preproposal contact when possible, and expand your network of informal links, you can be fairly certain that your proposal's format will be acceptable to your prospective funding source and that someone will read it.

Two sample letter proposals are included for your review, one to a foundation and one to a corporation (Exhibits 13.1 and 13.2).

Exhibit 13.1

SAMPLE LETTER PROPOSAL TO A FOUNDATION

January 6, 1998

Ms. Elaine Finsterwald, Trustee
Smith Foundation
123 Money Place
Clotin, NC 28699

Dear Ms. Finsterwald:

The Smith Foundation is synonymous with the word *education*. Since 1927, your grants have provided creative solutions to the educational needs of young people in Jonesboro and our state. Your recent annual report highlights your commitment to increase family involvement and responsibility in education. The $1.5 million in grants you have awarded over the past three years to strengthen families clearly demonstrates your dedication and concern.

[If applicable, mention previous support to your school district or the number of children who have been touched by any past support. For example, "Your grant to renovate an elementary classroom into the Smith Computer Lab has directly touched the lives of over 5,000 students in four years. Scores on standardized tests have improved 40 percent." If the Smith Foundation has not funded education directly, show how their support for your school-based project relates to their interest in programs related to the welfare of children, improving family life, parental responsibility and involvement, and so on.]

Previous generations have progressed through our schools with the involvement and encouragement of teachers and parents. Today, classroom leaders lack much of the support they were accustomed to getting from parents. Today's educator must deal with parents working several jobs and must compete with television and video games for a child's time and attention.

How much time do children spend watching television versus doing homework? A study of 25,000 middle school children conducted by the Department of Education reported 21.4 hours per week of television versus 5.6 hours of homework (*Wall Street Journal,* March 1992). When asked if parents placed limits on television, two-thirds of the parents surveyed said yes, while two-thirds of the children said no. These results suggest that some parents may have a problem setting priorities for their children.

Other results of the study point to the deterioration of parental responsibility and involvement in educational activities. For instance, four out of five parents surveyed reported that they regularly discuss schoolwork with their children, while two out of three children said parents rarely or never discuss schoolwork with them. Apparently the breakdown in communication between parents and children is at crisis proportions.

The need exists to develop and implement programs that encourage parents to become involved in their children's education. This means more than just visiting the school. For example, the Department of Education study also showed that 50 percent of parents had visited their child's school for meetings, but only 33 percent had visited their child's classroom.

What happens when parents take responsibility for working with their children and their children's school?

- Students whose parents discuss schoolwork with them get higher grades.
- Restrictions on television viewing tend to boost grades.

(continued)

Exhibit 13.1 (continued)

While some adults may think that the way to improve education is to increase funding for schools, taxpayers in Harrison, Arkansas, do not. While national test scores for students in Harrison rank in the top 10 percent of the country, Harrison ranks 272d out of Arkansas's 327 school districts in education taxes (*USA Today,* November 18, 1991). The key is parental involvement. Parents volunteer for one hour a week at each of the town's elementary schools, and parents and teachers meet each year to establish education goals for the next year.

What can we do in Clotin to promote the sharing of education among schools, parents, and children? We propose to utilize technology and old-fashioned responsibility. For only $2 per student we will ask parents to sign on to involvement through a contract for support. Each month a contract will be completed by the teacher, parent, and student. The contract will be done on three-part carbonless paper and will outline what can be expected from each to encourage better use of both in-school and out-of-school time—use that reinforces the student's education. From homework to more educational choices in family entertainment, all those involved will seek to make sure that the student gets the most out of his or her time.

To help parents maintain better access to their child's teacher(s) and to reinforce the completion of homework, we will install a computer-based program in our schools that lists each child's homework assignments. In addition, parents and students can help themselves through use of a computer-based "homework help line." Even if parents do not have access to computers, the contract for education will provide a communication vehicle for them. The added benefit of technology will provide a whole new way for the three partners in education—parent, child, and teacher—to communicate and increase learning.

The attached Project Planner outlines each objective and the activities that will foster the changes we desire. From increasing test scores to promoting public and volunteer service, Clotin schools will provide the catalyst for the education and involvement of parents in their children's responsible use of out-of-school time.

We request a grant from the Smith Foundation of $20,000 to initiate this project. Based upon our preliminary work with the teachers and Parent Advisory Committee of Clotin Schools, we anticipate the involvement of 1,600 students, 460 parents, and 60 teachers. Your grant funds will represent an investment of $20 per person served for the first year of the project. We are also in the process of securing funds from the ABC Foundation, the DEF Telephone Company, and the XYZ Power Company. These groups have already committed to granting $40,000 for this project. Our school district will provide $6,000 of in-kind contributions to support the project.

The Clotin Elementary School is fortunate to have Renee Weathers as the project director. Ms. Weathers was named 1997 Outstanding Teacher of the Year by the State Education Department. She will be assisted by the Parents Advisory Committee, chaired by Sam Price. The Committee is supported by a group of 140 parents, who have already volunteered 200 hours to develop the program and this proposal.

Clotin schools' tax exempt status is _____, and our tax exempt number is _____.
Renee Weathers is available at 200-861-4000 to answer your questions and to provide additional information that will help you arrive at your funding decision.

Sincerely,

Attachment

Exhibit 13.2

SAMPLE LETTER PROPOSAL TO A CORPORATION

January 12, 1998

Clyde L. Baker
Contributions Officer
Widget Corporation
4321 Commercial Park
Rocker, NY 14570

Dear Mr. Baker:

John Allen, your marketing manager, advised me to contact you for consideration of a grant from Widget Corporation. John, who has volunteered over 100 hours to our Parents Advisory Committee, has told us of your company's interest in and efforts to promote responsible behavior in your employees and their families. It is with this common interest in mind that Casper Schools request a grant of $20,000 from the Widget Corporation for the Responsibility in Education through Academic Partners Program (REAP).

John Allen has been instrumental in guiding our schools' curriculum group toward understanding the changes technological advances have brought to Widget Corporation and how these changes influence what types of employees and skills your corporation will require in the future.

Technological advances have also brought changes to the family. Everything from health to educational achievement to parent/child communication has been affected by television, videos, and computer games.

We have learned in education that what children devote their time to determines the skills they develop. Unfortunately, our children are devoting an inordinate amount of time to television and computer games. A study of 25,000 middle school children conducted by the Department of Education revealed that the children surveyed spent an average of 5.6 hours per week on homework and 21.4 hours per week watching television. In addition, when asked if parents placed limits on television, two-thirds of the parents surveyed said yes, while two-thirds of the children said no.

We are not suggesting that television viewing is inherently bad. However, the amount of television children watch is one possible indication of the responsibility parents take for their children's "out-of-school" time and ultimately for their education.

A parent's responsible involvement in his or her child's education can also be evaluated by the time spent discussing schoolwork within the family and the type or quality of parental contact with the child's school. The Department of Education's study revealed some disturbing facts in these areas as well.

•   Four out of five parents surveyed reported that they regularly discussed schoolwork with their children, while two out of three children said they rarely or never discussed schoolwork with their parents.

•   Fifty percent of the parents surveyed reported visiting their child's school for meetings, while only 33 percent had visited their child's classroom.

When you compare what can result from parental involvement and responsibility in education with what can result from a lack of parental involvement and responsibility in education, the problem is clear and the goal evident. Students whose parents discuss schoolwork with them get higher grades, and restrictions on television viewing tend to boost grades.

What can be done? This is the question that brought John Allen and over 100 other parents together to prepare a plan for action. The program they developed is entitled Responsibility in Education through Academic Partners (REAP).

(continued)

Exhibit 13.2 (continued)

REAP proposes to use technology and old-fashioned responsibility to promote the sharing of education among schools, parents, and children. For only $2 per student we will ask parents to sign on to involvement through a contract for support. Each month a contract will be completed by the teacher, parent, and student. The contract will be done on three-part carbonless paper and will outline what can be expected from each to encourage better use of both in-school and out-of-school time—use that reinforces the student's education. From homework to more educational choices in family entertainment, all those involved will seek to make sure that the student gets the most out of his or her time.

To help parents maintain better access to their child's teacher(s) and to reinforce the completion of homework, we will install a computer-based program in our schools that lists each child's homework assignments. In addition, parents and students can help themselves through use of a computer-based "homework help line." Even if parents do not have access to computers, the contract for education will provide a communication vehicle for them. The added benefit of technology will provide a whole new way for the three partners in education—parent, child, and teacher—to communicate and increase learning. The objectives of our project and the activities aimed at bringing about the desired changes are summarized on the enclosed Project Planner spreadsheet.

The Widget Corporation's support will be recognized in the REAP program's informational brochure, and space will be set aside on the brochure's inside cover for a statement from Widget Corporation.

Alice Jones has been selected as the project director. She is eminently qualified and has worked with parents in this region for over twenty-five years. As a sign of commitment, the school district has agreed to provide support services valued at $6,000.

The volunteers have done all they can do. The time is right. Please join with us in sowing the seeds for responsible, parental involvement in education.

Money alone does not ensure a great education. Responsible commitment does. In Harrison, Arkansas, national test scores ranked among the top 10 percent in the country, while education taxes rank 272nd out of Arkansas's 327 school districts. What's the key? Parental involvement. Approximately 10 parents volunteer one hour per week at each of the town's elementary schools, and parents and teachers work together each year to determine the following year's educational goals.

This project is truly an investment in our community. Alice Jones is ready to provide any additional information you may need to make your funding decision. Please call her at 321-987-0645. Our schools' tax exempt status is _____ and our tax exempt number is _____.

Sincerely,

Chapter 14

Improving and Submitting Your Foundation/Corporate Proposal

THE RESEARCH YOU HAVE COLLECTED on your prospective funding source reveals deadline dates for submitting your proposal if there are any. Some grantors have no deadlines. Proposals are read periodically or as needed. If there is a deadline, submit your proposal slightly early. This will eliminate the need for special delivery or express mail service, but you may still want to send your proposal by one of these means so that you can obtain a signed receipt for delivery to assure you that your proposal made it to the right place.

However you decide to send your proposal, conduct a mock review before submission to increase your chances of funding. As with federal grants opportunities, you want to be sure you are submitting a proposal that embodies your best effort and reflects well on you and your school.

Organizing a Proposal Improvement Group

Invite four or five people to form a group to help you improve your proposal. Ask a variety of individuals to participate—parents, students, educators, foundation or corporate board members, and anyone else you would like to involve in helping you develop your proposal. Note that a foundation or corporate board member can provide particularly valuable insight into the private grants review and decision-making process. Just be aware that once your volunteers realize how easy it is to develop a quality proposal for a foundation or corporation, they will want to take responsibility for more and more components of the proposal development process!

Mock reviews are much easier to perform for foundation and corporate proposals than for federal grant applications. First, it's fun to play the role of a wealthy and educated foundation or corporate board member. And second, it takes less time to read and make comments on foundation and corporate proposals than federal proposals because they are generally shorter.

Basically, you will be asking the four or five individuals invited to participate in your proposal improvement group to meet to conduct a mock review of your proposal that will be as much as possible like the actual review.

In most cases, the group members will spend only five to ten minutes reviewing the proposal. The entire evaluation process will be completed in less than one hour. If you will be submitting your proposal to a large foundation that has a required format and hires experts who spend more than one hour reviewing each proposal, ask your volunteers to review, comment on, and score your proposal before they meet as a group. The best way to find out about the review process of large corporations is to request the information in preproposal contact.

Proposal Improvement Scoring Worksheet

Complete the Foundation/Corporate Proposal Improvement Scoring Worksheet (Exhibit 14.1) in advance of your group meeting. Eventually you will make a copy of the worksheet for each group participant and distribute the worksheets at the meeting.

Record any information you have been able to uncover on the worksheet. This includes, but is not limited to, who reads the proposals, how much time will be spent reviewing each, the scoring system or criteria used for evaluation, and research on the grants history of the grantor.

Unfortunately, in most cases you will not have much information to record. Remember, private grant funds are not public money; therefore, private grantors are not required to provide you with information on the review process. In addition, most private grantors do not use an elaborate scoring or evaluation system.

What about background information on private funding officials? You can get some information from resource books such as *Who's Who* and *Standard and Poor's Register of Directors and Executives.* You should at least be able to provide your group members with the officials' ages and educational backgrounds and sometimes with brief biographies.

Give the volunteers a description of the funding source and any information you have on the types and numbers of proposals it has funded. If the funding source is a foundation, a copy of its IRS tax return will also help your group members. At the beginning of the meeting review the

---

Exhibit 14.1

FOUNDATION/CORPORATE PROPOSAL IMPROVEMENT SCORING WORKSHEET

The following information is being provided to help you review the attached foundation/corporate grant application/proposal.

The Proposal Will Be Read by:

_____ funding official   _____ board members

_____ funding staff   _____ other _____

_____ review committee

Amount of Time Spent Reviewing Each Proposal:

_____

Background of Reviewer(s):

College degrees (majors)_____

Socioeconomic background—upper class, middle class, etc. _____

_____

Known Viewpoints and Past Granting History:

Who has been funded for what types of projects and for what amounts of money? _____

_____

_____

_____

Positive Points   **Rank Order**

Negative Points   **Rank Order**

Other Comments/Suggestions for Improvement:

---

information to be sure the group members have a good idea of the grantor's point of view.

If you are in doubt about how much time the grantor spends reading each proposal, use a five-minute time limit. Even when your knowledge of the grantor is limited, a mock review is still an excellent investment of time when you consider the potential benefits.

Ask your volunteers to read the proposal quickly and to designate areas that they think will appeal to the grantor with a plus sign (+) and areas that need improvement with a minus sign (–). At the end of the five minutes, ask one volunteer to act as the recorder and to list the positive points on the worksheet. Ask the participants to briefly discuss the positive points and then to rank them, starting with the most positive. Have them repeat this procedure for the negative points. Finally, ask the participants to list suggestions for improvement.

In order not to impede the group's free expression, it would be best if you leave the room after naming the recorder. Don't worry—the ranking of the positive and negative areas will tell you how strongly the mock reviewers felt about specific parts of your proposal. This information plus the group's list of suggestions for improvement will give you valuable food for thought as you rewrite your proposal and put the finishing touches on your final version.

Chapter 15

Dealing with the Decision and Building Your Grantseeking Base

Sending off a grant proposal may be a great relief to all who helped create it, but it is not the end of the process. Reacting to and following up on the funder's decision—whether it be a rejection or an acceptance—is essential and is part of the effort you should make to build your grantseeking base.

Federal Grant Rejections

When a proposal is rejected, a grantseeker's first reaction is to withdraw from grantseeking and go into hibernation. Okay, you worked hard and you did not win. But you must act proactively, as you did when you began the grants process. After all, you knew when you started that not everyone ends up a winner. Remember that even grantseekers who are successful 50 percent of the time fail the other 50 percent. There are not enough federal grant funds to support all of even the best projects. You must now make a rational decision about whether you should resubmit your proposal. Review the following suggestions and keep your feelings in check.

Immediately send a thank-you letter to the federal agency official you have been in contact with. Thank the official for her help and let her know that you understand the agency's funding constraints. Ask to be sent your reviewers' comments and include a self-addressed label. Explain that your grants research indicated that the agency's program presented a great opportunity for funding because of its concern for your area of interest. Inform her that you will be contacting the agency in the near future concerning the next submission date and grants cycle. Ask if she anticipates the availability of any unsolicited funds or if there is any chance that one of the successful applicants may not expend all of the granted monies in the time allowed. You could use unexpended funds or unsolicited funding to do part of your project, which would make you a better applicant in the future.

Keep in contact with the funding source! Get ready for next year. Your chances may actually be better after you have been rejected because the reviewers' comments and insights will help you improve your proposal. Demonstrate a positive attitude and a sincere concern for the funder.

If you receive a letter that gives you a priority score and explains that you are not yet rejected but that the score is not adequate to attract funding, do not be a spoiler and protest it. Do not take the rejection personally. React constructively and positively and do not burn any bridges or alienate any funders. If you resubmit, your proposal is supposed to be judged by a new panel of reviewers, which means that you have a new chance of being funded. Try to be objective and rational about the likelihood of your project being funded upon resubmittal. If your score was very low, ask the grantor if it would be best for you to develop a whole new approach.

Federal Grant Acceptances

Many federal program officers who grant millions of dollars each year never receive thank-you letters or requests for reviewers' comments. (In many cases, applicants do not receive reviewers' comments unless they request this valuable feedback in writing.)

Be different. Send a thank-you letter and ask for the reviewers' comments. Include a self-addressed label. Remember, you need to know what you did that resulted in your high ranking so you can repeat the techniques. In addition, invite the granting officials to visit your school. They have the legal authority to make a site visit, but it looks better if you invite them.

Foundation and Corporate Rejections

The private grantor normally does not have the resources or support system necessary to provide you with reviewers' comments and scores. Because private grant funds do not come from tax dollars, you have no right to this information. As you probably will not receive much feedback, you may decide it best not to ask for it.

Send the foundation or corporation a thank-you letter. Say that you will reapply for funds unless advised not to. In the worst-case scenario, the grantor's decision makers meet once a year. When they gather to review grant applications, they will find your thank-you letter from last year and a new request for this year. Tell them that you understand that they limit their staff so they can use their resources on grants instead of payroll. You will not lose anything by sincerely thanking them for their time and the opportunity to compete for their grant funds. You might even invite them to visit your school. But you must face the fact that some of your proposals will be rejected. Make the best of the situation. Be positive and resubmit.

Foundation and Corporate Acceptances

You may receive a phone call or a letter informing you of your good fortune. Some foundations meet so infrequently and have such a limited staff that you will actually receive a check for your full request with the notification of your award. Immediately send a thank-you letter. Invite the grantor to visit your school and ask if it would like a presentation made by your students, teachers, or parents or a short video on your project to show at a future board meeting. Request comments on your proposal, including negative as well as positive feedback.

Nonprofit Organizations and Associations

When your request for a grant is denied by an association, civic group, or fraternal club, it is even more important to send a thank-you letter than it is with federal, foundation, or corporate grantors. You are likely to see these grantors in your school and community again and again. Say thanks and ask for suggestions for improvement and directions for resubmittal. Point out that the problem will not go away by itself and tell them that they will be hearing from you again. These funders interpret persistence as commitment, and you *are* a committed educator and community member.

If your proposal has been accepted, remember that voluntary organizations, service clubs, and fraternal groups like to keep their members and donors informed about educational changes they support. Send a thank-you letter to them immediately upon receiving word about your grant award and volunteer to make a presentation at their meeting or conference. Including your students in the presentation will make it even better.

Following Up with Federal Grantors

Follow-up with federal granting agencies can be divided into two basic categories: contact with the funder *while* your proposal is being reviewed and contact with the funder *after* the proposal outcome has been announced.

Contact During Review

A federal agency will consider contact from you during the period between the deadline and notification of the outcome as an attempt to influence the review and scoring system. Therefore, when your proposal is in submission, you should contact the funder only on the rare occasion when you must forward information of major significance: a new scientific breakthrough that will allow you to cut the price of budgeted equipment drastically, another grantor partially funding the project so that you want to reduce the amount of your request, or your need to withdraw the grant request. Lacking one of these three drastic reasons, stay away from the grantor while your proposal is being reviewed! This includes any intervention or contact by elected officials.

Contact After the Proposal Outcome Announcement

Unfortunately, many funding officials hear from prospective grantees only at the time of submittal. Actually, they should hear from grantees early in the funding cycle and again after the proposals have been reviewed. Contact the funder after your proposal outcome has been determined, whether your grant has been accepted or rejected.

Follow-up after acceptance is necessary to arrange the transfer of funds, site visits, and so on. How you will operate your grant depends on the system your district uses. It is crucial that you receive instructions on how to gain access to your grant funds and that your record keeping and hiring and purchasing procedures comply with federal guidelines.

Most school districts have to deal with federal programs on an ongoing basis and therefore have all the necessary procedures in place. There are two basic transfer systems for providing grantees access to their federal grant monies. The first is for the grantee to provide a cash forecast to the federal granting agency and for the federal grantor to send the money in advance, based on the needs outlined in the forecast. In your case, funds would be sent to your school district before grant expenditures were made. In the second transfer system, the grantee pays all proposal expenses up front, and the federal grantor reimburses the grantee after the fact. In other words, your district would pay your proposal expenses up front and the federal grantor would reimburse the district after the expenditures were made. In either case, you need to know who handles the funds in your district and how you can gain access to them.

In addition, you should develop a system for keeping track of any reports required by the federal granting agency. You may have agreed to send it progress indicators, milestones, or products. Keep in contact, comply with report requirements and deadlines, and meet all of your responsibilities in a timely manner.

Following Up with Foundation and Corporate Grantors

Follow-up with foundations and corporations that have no staff and rarely meet is very difficult. Still, mail them materials that point out or highlight their interests. Send pictures or news releases that demonstrate what you have accomplished with their funds and with the support of other funding sources.

Building Your Grantseeking Base

Continue to build your base of likely funders for your school and classroom projects. File your project ideas and useful news and research articles in your Grants Workbook (see Chapter Two).

Keep up your webbing and linkage contacts. Stay alert for contacts that can provide access to granting officials. Once you get the ball rolling, the grants process will become more and more familiar to you and easier to control.

The biggest danger you can encounter in grantseeking is success. It may distract you from your primary focus: teaching. If you do not mind being called from your classroom to assist other educators who want grantseeking information, you have nothing to worry about. But be forewarned: the concepts in this primer work. Use them and you will succeed. The funds you generate will increase your power and influence but, most important, the benefits to your students, your school, and your community will be phenomenal. Good luck!

Bibliography

Government Grant Resources

Commerce Business Daily

The government's contracts publication, published five times a week, the *Daily* announces every government Request for Proposal (RFP) that exceeds $25,000 and upcoming sales of government surplus. **Price:** $275 annually for domestic, $324 for first class; $137 domestic for six months, $162 for first class. **Order from:** Superintendent of Documents, PO Box 371954, Pittsburgh, PA 15250-7954, 202-512-1800, fax 202-512-2250, website www.access.gpo.gov/su_docs/

Catalog of Federal Domestic Assistance (CFDA)

This is the government's most complete listing of federal domestic assistance programs with details on eligibility, application procedures, and deadlines, including the location of state plans. It is published at the beginning of each fiscal year with supplementary updates during the year. Indexes are by agency program, function, popular name, applicant eligibility, and subject. It comes in looseleaf form, punched for a three-ring binder. **Price:** $72 annual subscription. **Order from:** Superintendent of Documents, PO Box 371954, Pittsburgh, PA 15250-7954, 202-512-1800, fax 202-512-2250, website www.access.gpo.gov/su_docs/

The Federal Register

Published five times a week (Monday through Friday), the *Register* supplies up-to-date information on federal assistance and supplements the *Catalog of Federal Domestic Assistance (CFDA)*. It includes public regulations and legal notices issued by all federal agencies and presidential proclamations. Of particular importance are the proposed rules, final rules, and program deadlines. An index is published monthly. **Price:** $555 per year. **Order from:** Superintendent of Documents, PO Box 371954, Pittsburgh, PA 15250-7954, 202-512-1800, fax 202-512-2250, website www.access.gpo.gov/su_docs/

United States Government Manual

This paperback manual gives the names of key personnel, addresses, and telephone numbers for all agencies and departments that constitute the federal bureaucracy. **Price:** $40 per year. **Order from:** Superintendent of Documents, PO Box 371954, Pittsburgh, PA 15250-7954, 202-512-1800, fax 202-512-2250, website www.access.gpo.gov/su_docs/

Academic Research Information System, Inc. (ARIS)

ARIS provides timely information about grant and contract opportunities, including concise descriptions of guidelines and eligibility requirements, upcoming deadlines, identification of program resource persons, and new program policies for both government and nongovernment funding sources.

Biomedical Sciences Report $240

Social and Natural Science Report $240

Arts and Humanities Report $145

All three ARIS Reports and Supplements $575

Order from: Academic Research Information System, Inc., The Redstone Building, 2940 16th Street, Suite 314, San Francisco, CA 94103, 415-558-8133, fax 415-558-8135, e-mail arisnet@dnai.com, website www:arisnet.com

Federal Grants and Contracts Weekly

This weekly contains information on the latest Requests for Proposals (RFPs), contracting opportunities, and upcoming grants. Each ten-page issue includes details on RFPs, closing dates for grant programs, procurement-related news, and newly issued regulations. **Price:** $389 for 50 issues. **Order from:** Capitol Publications, Inc., 1101 King Street, PO Box 1453, Alexandria, VA 22313-2053, 800-655-5597, fax 703-739-6437, website www.grantscape.com

Health Grants and Contracts Weekly

Price: $379 for 50 issues. **Order from:** Capitol Publications, Inc., 1101 King Street, PO Box 1453, Alexandria, VA 22313-2053, 800-655-5597, fax 703-739-6437, website www.grantscape.com

Education Daily

Price: $598 for 250 issues. **Order from:** Capitol Publications, Inc., 1101 King Street, PO Box 1453, Alexandria, VA 22313-2053, 800-655-5597, fax 703-739-6437, website www.grantscape.com

Education Grants Alert
Price: $399 for 50 issues. **Order from:** Capitol Publications, Inc., 1101 King Street, PO Box 1453, Alexandria, VA 22313-2053, 800-655-5597, fax 703-739-6437, website www.educationdaily.com

Washington Information Directory, 1998/1999
This directory is divided into three categories: agencies of the executive branch, Congress, and private or "nongovernmental" organizations. Each entry includes the name, address, telephone number, and director of the organization and a short description of its work. **Price:** $110.00. **Order from:** Congressional Quarterly Books, 1414 22nd NW, Washington, DC 20037, 800-638-1710, fax 800-380-3810, e-mail bookhelp@cqualert.com

Foundation Grant Resources

Many of the following research aids can be found through the Foundation Center Cooperating Collections Network. If you wish to purchase any of the following Foundation Center publications, contact: The Foundation Center, 79 Fifth Avenue, Dept. VL, New York, NY 10003-3076, 800-424-9836. In NY State: 212-807-3690, fax 212-807-3677, website www.fdncenter.org

Corporate Foundation Profiles, 10th edition, 1998
This Foundation Center publication contains detailed analyses of 195 of the largest corporate foundations in the United States. An appendix lists financial data on 1,000 smaller corporate grantmakers. **Price:** $155. **Order from:** The Foundation Center

The Foundation 1,000, 1997/1998 Edition
This research aid profiles the 1,000 largest U.S. foundations by foundation name, subject field, type of support, and geographic location. There is also an index that allows you to target grantmakers by the names of officers, staff, and trustees. **Price:** $295. **Order from:** The Foundation Center

The Foundation Directory, 1998 Edition
This is the most important single reference work available on grantmaking foundations in the United States. It includes information on foundations having assets of at least $2 million or annual grants exceeding $200,000. Each entry includes a description of giving interests, along with address, telephone numbers, current financial data, names of donors, and contact person, and IRS identification number. Includes six indexes: state and city, subject, foundation donors, trustees and administrators, and alphabetical foundation names. The trustees index is very valuable in

developing linkages to decision makers. **Price:** $215 hardcover. $185 softcover. **Order from:** The Foundation Center

The Foundation Directory Supplement, 1998

The *Supplement* updates the *Directory* so that users will have the latest addresses, contacts, policy statements, application guidelines, and financial data. **Price:** $125. $320 hardcover: *Directory* and *Supplement*. $290 softcover: *Directory* and *Supplement*. **Order from:** The Foundation Center

The Foundation Directory Part 2, 1998 Edition

This *Directory* provides information on over 4,900 midsize foundations with grant programs between $50,000 and $200,000. Published biennially. **Price:** $185. $485 hardcover: *Directory, Supplement, Part 2*. $455 softcover: *Directory, Supplement, Part 2*. **Order from:** The Foundation Center

The Foundation Grants Index, 1998 Edition

This cumulative listing of over 73,000 grants of $10,000 or more made by over 1,000 major foundations is indexed by subject and geographic locations, by the names of recipient organizations, and by key words. **Price:** $165. **Order from:** The Foundation Center

Foundation Grants to Individuals, 10th Edition, 1997

Comprehensive listing of over 3,200 independent and corporate foundations that provide financial assistance to individuals. **Price:** $65. **Order from:** The Foundation Center

The National Guide to Funding for Elementary and Secondary Education, 4th Edition, 1997

Includes over 2,300 sources of funding for elementary and secondary education and over 6,300 grant descriptions listing the organizations that have successfully approached these funding sources. **Price:** $140. **Order from:** The Foundation Center

Education Grant Guides, 1997/1998 Editions

There are seven Grant Guides in the field of education, including: Elementary and Secondary Education, Higher Education, Libraries and Information Services, Literacy, Reading and Adult/Continuing Education, Scholarships, Student Aid and Loans, Science and Technology Programs, and Social and Political Science Programs. There are twenty-four other guides in areas other than education, such as children and youth, alcohol and drug abuse, minorities, and the like. Each guide has a customized list of hundreds of recently awarded grants of $10,000 or more. Sources of funding are indexed by type of organization, subject focus, and geographic funding area. **Price:** $75 each. **Order from:** The Foundation Center

The Taft Foundation Information System
Foundation Reporter: This annual directory of the largest private charitable foundations in the United States supplies descriptions and statistical analyses. $400.

Foundation Giving Watch: This monthly publishes news and the "how-to's" of foundation giving, with a listing of recent grants. Yearly subscription $149. **Order from:** Taft Group, 835 Penobscot Building, Detroit, MI 48226, 800-877-8238, fax 800-414-5043, website www.gale.com

Foundation and Corporate Grants Alert
Price: $297 for 12 issues. **Order from:** Capitol Publications, Inc., 1101 King Street, PO Box 1453, Alexandria, VA 22313-2053, 800-655-5597, fax 703-739-6437, website www.grantscape.com

Private Foundation IRS Tax Returns
(Available from the IRS or free to use at Foundation Center)
The Internal Revenue Service requires private foundations to file income tax returns each year. Form 990-PF provides fiscal details on receipts and expenditures, compensation of officers, capital gains or losses, and other financial matters. Form 990-AR provides information on foundation managers, assets, and grants paid or committed for future payment. The IRS makes this information available on aperture cards that may be viewed at libraries operated by the Foundation Center or at its regional cooperating collections. You may also obtain this information by writing to the appropriate IRS office (see accompanying list). Enclose as much information about the foundation as possible, including its full name, street address with zip code, its employer identification number if available, and the year or years requested. It generally takes four to six weeks for the IRS to respond, and it will bill you for all charges, which vary depending on the office and number of pages involved.

INTERNATIONAL REVENUE SERVICE CENTER REGIONAL OFFICES

Central Region (Indiana, Kentucky, Michigan, Ohio, West Virginia)
Public Affairs Officer, Internal Revenue Service Center, PO Box 1699, Cincinnati, OH 45201

Mid-Atlantic Region (District of Columbia, Maryland, Virginia, Pennsylvania—Zip Codes 150–168 and 172)
Public Affairs Officer, Internal Revenue Service Center, 11601 Roosevelt Blvd., Philadelphia, PA 19154

Midwest Region (Illinois, Iowa, Minnesota, Missouri, Montana, Nebraska, North Dakota, Oregon, South Dakota, Wisconsin)

Public Affairs Officer, Internal Revenue Service Center, PO Box 24551, Kansas City, MO 64131

North Atlantic Region (Connecticut, Delaware, Maine, Massachusetts, New Hampshire, New York, New Jersey, Rhode Island, Vermont, Pennsylvania—Zip Codes 169–171 and 173–196)

Public Affairs Officer, Internal Revenue Service Center, PO Box 400, Brookhaven, NY 11742

Southeast Region (Alabama, Arkansas, Georgia, Florida, Louisiana, Mississippi, North Carolina, South Carolina, Tennessee)

Public Affairs Officer, Internal Revenue Service Center, PO Box 47-421, Doraville, GA 30362

Southwest Region (Arizona, Colorado, Kansas, New Mexico, Oklahoma, Texas, Utah, Wyoming)

Public Affairs Officer, Internal Revenue Service Center, PO Box 934, Austin, TX 78767

Western Region (Alaska, California, Hawaii, Idaho, Nevada, Washington)

Public Affairs Officer, Internal Revenue Service Center, PO Box 12866, Fresno, CA 93779

Corporate Grant Resources

Annual Survey of Corporate Contributions

This annual survey of corporate giving is sponsored by the Conference Board and the Council for Financial Aid to Education. It includes a detailed analysis of beneficiaries of corporate support but does not list individual firms and specific recipients. **Price:** $30 for Associates. $120 for Nonassociates. **Order from:** The Conference Board, 845 Third Avenue, New York, NY 10022, 212-759-0900, fax 212-980-7014, website www.conference-board.org

The National Directory of Corporate Giving, 5th Edition

This directory provides information on over 1,905 corporate foundations plus an additional 990 direct, corporate giving programs. It also has an extensive bibliography and six indexes to help you target funding prospects. **Price:** $225. **Order from:** The Foundation Center, 79 Fifth Avenue, Dept. VL, New York, NY 10003-3076, 800-424-9836. In NY State 212-807-3690

Directory of Corporate Affiliations

This directory lists divisions, subsidiaries, and affiliates of thousands of companies with addresses, telephone numbers, key persons, employees, etc. **Price:** $1029.95 plus handling and delivery. **Order from:** Reed Elsevier,

PO Box 31, New Providence, NJ 07974, 800-323-6772, fax 908-665-6688, website www.bowker.com

Dun and Bradsteet's Million Dollar Directory, 5 volumes
The five volumes list names, addresses, employees, sales volume, and other pertinent data for 160,000 of America's largest businesses. **Price:** $1,445 for 5 volumes. **Order from:** Dun and Bradstreet Information Services, 3 Sylvan Way, Parsippany, NJ 07054, 800-526-0651, fax 973-605-6911, website www.dnbmdd.com

Standard and Poor's Register of Corporations, Directors and Executives
This annual register provides up-to-date rosters of over 400,000 executives of the 77,000 nationally known corporations they represent, with their names, titles, and business affiliations. **Price:** $749 for one year, includes quarterly supplements. **Order from:** Standard and Poor's Corporation, 25 Broadway, 17th Floor, Attn: Sales, New York, NY 10004, 212-208-8000

Taft Corporate Giving Directory, 1998 Edition
This directory provides detailed entries on 1,000 corporate foundations. Included are nine indexes. **Price:** $425 plus postage and handling. **Order from:** Taft Group, 838 Penobscot Building, Detroit, MI 48226, 800-877-8238, fax 800-414-5043, website www.gale.com

Corporate Giving Watch
This monthly reports on corporate giving developments. **Price:** $149 a year. **Order from:** Taft Group, 838 Penobscot Building, Detroit, MI 48226, 800-877-8238, fax 800-414-5043, website www.gale.com

Computer Research Services

Congressional Information Service Index (CIS Index)
CIS covers congressional publications and legislation from 1970 to date. It covers hearings, committee prints, House and Senate reports and documents, special publications, Senate executive reports and documents, and public laws. It includes monthly abstracts and index volumes. Noncomputer grant-related materials are also available from CIS, including a CIS Federal Register Index, which covers announcements from the Federal Register on a weekly basis. **Price:** Sliding scale. Call for quote. **Order from:** Congressional Information Services, Inc., 4520 East-West Highway, Suite 800, Bethesda, MD 20814, 800-638-8380, fax 301-951-4660, website www.cispubs.com

DIALOG Information Services
3460 Hillview Avenue, Palo Alto, CA 94304, 800-334-2564. A commercial organization that provides access to hundreds of databases in a range of

subject areas. DIALOG has no start-up fees or monthly minimum charges, but there is an annual fee. Foundation Center files also have a cost per minute to search on-line. Each full record printed off-line or by DIALOG has an additional cost.

Federal Assistance Program Retrieval System (FAPRS)
The *FAPRS* lists more than 1,300 federal grant programs, including planning and technical assistance. There is a $53 hookup fee. All states have *FAPRS* services available through state, county, and local agencies as well as through federal extension services. For further information, call 202-708-5126 or write to:

1. Your congressperson's office; it can request a search for you, in some cases at no charge.

2. Federal Domestic Assistance Catalog Staff, GSA/IRMS/WKU, 300 7th Street SW, Reporters Building, Room 101, Washington, DC 20407, fax 202-401-8233, website www.gsa.gov/fdac

Foundation Center Databases
The Foundation Center maintains two databases on DIALOG, one on grantmakers and the other on the grants they distribute. For more information contact DIALOG at 800-334-2564 or the Foundation Center's DIALOG support staff at 212-807-3690.

The Sponsored Programs Information Network (SPIN)
This is a database of federal and private funding sources. **Price:** Call for quote or visit its website. **Order from:** InfoEd, 2301 Western Ave., Guilderland, NY 12084, 518-464-0691, fax 518-464-0695, website www.infoed.org

FC Search: The Foundation Center's Database on CD-ROM, Version 2.0
This fund-raising CD-ROM covers over 45,000 foundations and corporate givers, includes descriptions of nearly 200,000 associated grants, and lists over 183,000 trustees, officers, and donors. **Price:** Stand-alone (single user) version $1,195; Network (2–8 users at a single site) $1,495. Prices include one user manual. Additional copies of user manuals are $19.95 each. **Order from:** The Foundation Center, 79 Fifth Avenue, New York, NY 10003-3076, 800-424-9836. In NY State 212-807-3690.